Shaky Ground

The Strange Saga of the U.S. Mortgage Giants

COLUMBIA GLOBAL REPORTS
NEW YORK

Shaky Ground
The Strange Saga of the U.S. Mortgage Giants

Bethany McLean

United
States

Des Moines, Iowa

Washington, D.C.

0 Miles   2,500

0 Kilometers 2,500

Scale at latitude of Washington, D.C.

Published by Columbia Global Reports
91 Claremont Avenue, Suite 515
New York, New York 10027
http://globalreports.columbia.edu/
facebook.com/columbiaglobalreports
@columbiaGR

Library of Congress Control Number: 2015940135
ISBN: 978-0-9909763-0-1

Book design by Strick&Williams
Map design by Jeffrey L. Ward
Author photograph credit: Steven Laxton

Printed in the United States of America

© 2015 Jeffrey L. Ward

CONTENTS

Preface

What are the risks remaining to the global financial system in the wake of the crisis of 2008? I have thought a lot about this topic, but I've always believed that trying to forecast the cause of the next meltdown is an exercise in futility. One rule about financial crises that seems to hold true is that the spark that lights the fire is never what everyone, or even anyone, was expecting.

Nevertheless, there is a big issue left over from the darkest days of the financial crisis, and while it might not be the cause of an imminent meltdown, it is a festering problem. That is what to do about Fannie Mae and Freddie Mac, the mortgage giants that the U.S. government took over in the fall of 2008 by putting them into "conservatorship," a state in which they are supported by a line of credit from the Treasury and effectively run by a government agency. We were supposed to figure out how to resolve these controversial companies—collectively called the GSEs, for government-sponsored enterprises—and maybe even to push RESTART on the role that the government has long played in promoting and supporting America's cult of home-ownership. But here we are, seven years after Fannie and Freddie were taken over. The big banks have at least superficially paid back the money the government gave them; General Motors and Chrysler are out of bankruptcy; but Fannie and Freddie are still in conservatorship. Even more significant, most of the mortgage market in this country is now supported by government agencies, more so than it was before the financial crisis. The former governor of the Bank of England, Mervyn King, told me this: "Most countries have socialized health care and a free market for mortgages. You in the United States do exactly the opposite."

It's a strange state of affairs—but I've come to believe that in the world of Fannie and Freddie, strange is actually normal. Start with the fact that although these two companies touch the lives of almost every American who has a mortgage and even many who rent—they determine who gets mortgage credit and at what price, especially today—very few people understand what they do. They are part of the hidden machinery of the world that makes our lives, in this case our financial lives, possible, but which we never think about—or won't until there's a problem. Another oddity about these companies is that while homes are the most domestic asset possible, Fannie and Freddie are global, because through their securities, foreign investors, including China's central bank, finance the purchase of Americans' homes. This seems like a good thing—it's globalization at work!—but, as the story of Fannie and Freddie shows, it has also tied the hands of the government at critical times.

10   The story really is a saga, with all sorts of unexpected twists and turns, and conspiracy theories galore. "You can't make this stuff up," a longtime lobbyist once told me. "The GSE world is a cross between Monty Python and Shakespeare." Right now, a group of investors is suing the U.S. government over how it has handled Fannie and Freddie, and while you might think that the investors, which are mostly powerful hedge funds, are only looking after their own dollar—and they are—I've also come to believe that they're looking after the rest of us by providing a check on the government's behavior that otherwise wouldn't exist.

I first started writing about the GSEs in 2004, when Fannie had an accounting scandal. Even though I'd been covering business for almost a decade at that point, I still couldn't believe that anything like Fannie and Freddie existed. They were (and are) unimaginably gigantic companies that were like mythical beasts— part government agencies and part normal companies, with shareholders and boards of directors. There was always an argument that this sort of public-private partnership, which harnessed the power of the government to the discipline of the market, was the best of all possible worlds. But at the time I wrote about Fannie, I was convinced that it was a bad actor. When Fannie executives argued that their enemies just wanted to turn their business over to the big banks, along with their profits, I thought that was just a conspiracy theory. And even if I had believed it, I would have thought, "Well, what's wrong with that?" I too was a believer in what Franklin Raines, Fannie's former CEO, calls "marketification": the idea that the free market fixes all.

That was long before the financial crisis, about which even Alan Greenspan, that ardent believer in Ayn Rand's libertarianism, said in 2008: "Those of us who have looked to the self-interest of lending institutions to protect shareholders' equity, myself included, are in a state of shocked disbelief." There were lots of villains in the run-up to the financial crisis, which is why Joe Nocera and I titled our 2010 book *All the Devils Are Here*. And while Fannie and Freddie were two of the villains, by no means were they the only ones. I would have liked to have blamed the financial crisis on them—there would be much more clarity that way, and we'd be able to keep the religion that is marketification alive—but I have never been able to make the facts line up with that narrative.

I've never found any simple way to summarize what I think about the GSEs, although I have come to my own view about where we are today and where we should go. I don't think everyone should agree with me. But I do think everyone should care. What I've tried to do in this book is to lay out the facts in a way that I hope will help readers think about the issues and make up their own minds. This is too important to let special interests determine the outcome while we all play possum.

12   CAST OF CHARACTERS

Fannie Mae
Jim Johnson
CEO, 1991–1998

Franklin Raines
CEO, 1999–2004

Daniel Mudd
CEO, 2005–2008

Timothy Mayopoulos
CEO, 2012–current

Timothy Howard
CFO, 1990–2004

Thomas Lund
Executive Vice President of
Single-Family Mortgage Business
2005-2009

Freddie Mac
Leland Brendsel
CEO, 1987–2003

Richard Syron
CEO, 2003–2007

Federal Housing Finance Agency
Ed DeMarco
Director, 2009–2014

Mel Watt
Director, 2014–current

**Office of Federal Housing
Enterprise Oversight**
Jim Lockhart
Director, 2006–2008;
Director of the FHFA, 2008–2009

Armando Falcon
Director, 1999–2005

White House
Henry Paulson
Secretary of the Treasury,
2006–2009

Timothy Geithner
Secretary of the Treasury,
2009–2013

Lawrence Summers
Director of the National Economic
Council, 2009–2010

Gene Sperling
Director of the National Economic
Council, 2011–2014

Austan Goolsbee
Chairman of the Council of
Economic Advisers, 2010–2011

Federal Reserve
Ben Bernanke
Chairman, 2006–2014

Alan Greenspan
Chairman, 1987–2006

Paul Volcker
Chairman, 1979–1987

Marriner Eccles
Chairman, 1934–1948

Congress

Jeb Hensarling
Chairman of the House Financial
Services Committee, 2013—current

Barney Frank
Chairman of the House Financial
Services Committee, 2007—2011

Mark Warner
Democratic Senator of Virginia

Bob Corker
Republican Senator of Tennessee

Charles Schumer
Democratic Senator of New York

Courts

Robert Pratt
Senior District Judge, District Court
for the Southern District of Iowa

Royce Lamberth
Senior Judge, District Court for
the District of Columbia

Investors

Richard Perry
Founder of Perry Capital

Bruce Berkowitz
Founder and Chief Investment Officer
of Fairholme Capital Management

William Ackman
CEO of Pershing Square Capital
Management

Housing Activists

John Taylor
President of National Community
Reinvestment Coalition

Judy Kennedy
President and CEO of National
Association of Affordable Housing
Lenders, 1998—2015

Analysts

Peter Wallison
Scholar, American Enterprise
Institute; Member, Financial Crisis
Inquiry Commission

Ed Pinto
Scholar, American Enterprise
Institute

Mark Calabria
Director of Financial Regulation
Studies, Cato Institute

Yu Yongding
Member, Monetary Policy
Committee of the People's Bank
of China, 2004—2006

Laurie Goodman
Director, Housing Finance Policy
Center

Joshua Rosner
Managing Director,
Graham Fisher & Co.

14   LIST OF ACRONYMS

FNMA
Federal National
Mortgage Association,
or Fannie Mae

FHLMC
Federal Home Loan
Mortgage Corporation,
or Freddie Mac

GNMA
Government National
Mortgage Association,
or Ginnie Mae

GSE
Government-Sponsored
Enterprise

FHFA
Federal Housing
Finance Agency

FHA
Federal Housing
Administration

OFHEO
Office of Federal Housing
EnterpriseOversight

NEC
National Economic
Council

GAO
Government Accountability
Office

CBO
Congressional Budget
Office

HUD
Department of Housing
and Urban Development

SEC
Securities and Exchange
Commission

FCIC
Financial Crisis Inquiry
Commission

HERA
Housing and Economic
Recovery Act of 2008

PATH
Protecting American Taxpayers
and Homeowners Act

NHA
National Housing Act

NCRC
National Community
Reinvestment Coalition

RFC
Reconstruction Finance
Corporation

AIG
American International
Group

TARP
Troubled Asset Relief
Program

Introduction

"If the housing market tanks, so does the stock market. No matter who you are, this is hugely impactful. And no one is talking about it. No one realizes it."
—Ryan Israel, partner at Pershing Square Capital Management

On a bitterly cold gray day in December 2014, there was a strangely large crowd at the United States Courthouse in Des Moines, Iowa, where Senior District Judge Robert Pratt was hearing arguments in *Continental Western Insurance Company v. FHFA*. The title gave few hints as to why the room, the goings-on of which rarely transcend local interest, would be packed close to standing-room-only, filled with representatives of the country's top investment firms, including a slew of New York hedge fund types, along with prominent Washington lawyers, including a George W. Bush-appointed former U.S. Attorney and a Department of Justice lawyer.

FHFA, often pronounced "FOO-fa," is the acronym for the Federal Housing Finance Agency. It's an obscure government regulator whose major business is overseeing Fannie Mae and

16   Freddie Mac, the mortgage giants that guarantee the payments made by a broad swath of American homeowners, and which were taken over by the U.S. government during the financial crisis. Continental Western is an Iowa-based insurance company that coordinated its case with Fairholme Capital Management, the famous investment firm founded by Bruce Berkowitz. The case in the Iowa court is one of many that investors including Fairholme have brought against the government for the way it has handled Fannie and Freddie.

The government lawyers were sputtering with outrage about the nerve of the investors to bring a lawsuit at all. It's not just that investors are accusing the United States government of misdeeds, which in and of itself is obviously a pretty big deal. But on the surface, the lawsuits seem to fail to appreciate the stunning amount of money—$187 billion, or about six times the annual budget of the National Institutes of Health—that taxpayers have put into the rescue of Fannie and Freddie. And taxpayers still could have to contribute more. Said the FHFA's lawyer, "Your honor, even with that $187 billion already infused, at this very moment, Treasury . . . is on the hook to infuse another—if it is required—in excess of another $250 billion of taxpayer dollars, a quarter trillion dollars . . . all this federal money was put in and [the investors] want to avail themselves of that federal money."

A news service called the Capitol Forum described the Iowa case as a "match-up between the Obama Administration and hedge funds." And the legal battles over Fannie and Freddie's fate do pit the most powerful office in the land against some of the country's wealthiest investors. But overall, the lawsuits are

about much more than one side's victory or loss. They have reverberations for all of us.

Fannie Mae and Freddie Mac—officially, the Federal
National Mortgage Association and the Federal Home Loan
Mortgage Corporation—are critically important and very large
entities, with assets in the trillions of dollars, that were created
by Congress but for many years operated as something between
a private business and a government agency. They are meant to
serve the longstanding dream of the United States as a society
of individual homeowners; they do this by buying up, packag-
ing, and reselling in bulk millions of mortgages that ordinary
Americans take out from financial institutions. They are part of
the lives of almost every homeowner with a mortgage in this
country, and they are meant to generate a sense among investors that home mortgages are safe, because Fannie and Freddie,
which are sponsored by the government, stand behind them.

The United States was historically a pioneer, and an out-
lier in a global context, in putting into practice such democratic
ideas as universal voting, universal public education, and nearly
universal land or homeownership. In all these cases, American
society's big reach also generates big controversies, and in the
business of homeownership the controversies are both domestic policy battles—why do we need the government in our
mortgage markets at all?—and potential international policy
issues, because many billions of dollars of U.S. mortgage debt
are owned by other governments that very much want to see it
as a stable investment.

Most people who weren't paying close attention probably
date the beginning of the global financial crisis at September

15, 2008, the day Lehman Brothers declared bankruptcy. But a few days earlier, on September 6, the U.S. Treasury put Fannie Mae and Freddie Mac into a status called conservatorship, a kind of government life-support system hooked up because the rapidly swooning mortgage markets had arguably put Fannie and Freddie in mortal peril, and their failure would have caused global economic chaos. The Treasury gave Fannie and Freddie an immediate $200 billion line of credit. September 6 is probably a better start date for the final cataclysmic period of the long-brewing financial crisis than September 15. And, seven years later, the big banks that the government rescued at the height of the crisis are back to relatively normal operations, if they survived. Fannie and Freddie are not—and that's a problem.

The lawsuits have their roots in the aftermath of the crisis. Fannie and Freddie are publicly traded companies, and remained so even after the government put them in conservatorship, although their stock prices declined to near zero. In the darkest days, when most people thought the two companies would lose hundreds of billions of dollars, some of the country's most famous investors made a very contrarian bet: They would buy Fannie and Freddie stocks cheap, and then make a fortune on that investment after the two companies began producing profits again. And the two companies are indeed very profitable today. As of spring 2015, they have paid $231 billion back to the U.S. Treasury, or over $40 billion more than they got from taxpayers. The problem is that Fannie and Freddie are still in conservatorship, and the government in 2012 changed the terms of the bailout and is now directing almost all their profits toward reduction of the federal deficit. The investors think the government has broken the law, and that's why they are suing.

In total, the lawsuits, if successful, could result in the payment of tens of billions of dollars for securities that originally cost pennies; *Bloomberg* called it "one of the biggest potential paydays in history." But some investors are after even more than that. What they want is a say, and a stake, in the ultimate fate of Fannie and Freddie—and that, in turn, will decide the future structure of the American housing market.

Both Fannie and Freddie came into existence as part of a government effort to promote homeownership that is almost as old as this country. The notion that homeowners will make better, more responsible citizens and therefore will help create a more stable society has persisted over time and across the political spectrum, despite a lack of hard proof that it's true. Fannie, the older, bigger, and far more powerful of the two companies, was founded as a part of the New Deal. "The significance of a new housing program that could revive the economy was not lost on President Roosevelt," wrote Marriner Eccles, the chairman of the Federal Reserve under FDR and the ur-Keynesian before Keynes. "He knew that almost a third of the unemployed were to be found in the building trades. . . . [Housing] would act as the wheel within the wheel to move the whole economic engine." In the decades since, Eccles's words have only become more true.

Neither Fannie nor Freddie lends money directly to homebuyers. Instead, they buy mortgages that have been made by banks and other lenders. The original theory was that the ability to get cash—immediately—for existing loans freed up mortgage makers to go out and make more loans. Having a national

20 purchaser of mortgages also evened out the flow of credit in this huge, diverse country—or, as the International Directory of Company Histories described Fannie Mae's purpose, "In this way a Boston banker could invest in Arizona mortgages while a local lender in Arizona was no longer limited in the number of loans he could make by the cash deposits of his customer."

Originally, Fannie and Freddie owned the mortgages they purchased. But over time, as the capital markets in this country evolved, Fannie and Freddie began to package up the mortgages they purchased, stamp them with a guarantee that Fannie and Freddie would pay the interest and principle on the mortgages if the homeowners couldn't, and sell them as securities to investors. In essence, Fannie and Freddie are insurers, and insurers who offered an apparently gold-plated guarantee. Even before the Treasury's takeover, everyone believed that if there were a problem, the federal government would stand behind its government-sponsored enterprises, or GSEs, although officially, everyone denied that that was true.

In large part because of their perceived safety as an investment, American mortgages became catnip to global investors. By the 1990s, it wasn't just Boston bankers investing in Arizona mortgages, but Chinese workers and their savings accounts enabling Americans in Kansas to buy homes. By the 2000s, foreign central banks and other foreign investors were financing over a trillion dollars of American mortgage debt via their ownership of GSE securities.

It was Hank Paulson, the former Goldman Sachs executive who served as Treasury Secretary from 2006 until January 20, 2009, who orchestrated the government takeover of Fannie and Freddie during the financial crisis. Something that he says "took his breath away" happened during the summer of 2008, when he was at the Beijing Olympics. As Paulson wrote in his memoir, *On the Brink*, he heard at that time that the Russians made a "top-level approach" to the Chinese "suggesting that they might together sell big chunks of their GSE holdings to force the U.S. to use its emergency authorities to prop up these companies." (Russia has denied this.) Although Paulson said the Chinese declined, heavy selling of Fannie and Freddie securities would have reverberated throughout the already shaky financial system. Because the holders of Fannie and Freddie debt believed that the U.S. would come to their rescue, if the government had instead allowed investors to suffer losses on Fannie and Freddie debt, one of the consequences might have been questions about the creditworthiness of the United States itself.

When they were taken over, Fannie and Freddie had a combined $5.3 trillion in outstanding debt, which, had it been put on the government's balance sheet, would have increased the public national debt by about 50 percent. Partly to avoid that, the government left 20.1 percent of Fannie's common stock, as well as other securities known as preferred shares, in the hands of investors. That decision led directly to the drama in the Iowa courtroom.

What almost everyone expected was that the GSEs would long ago have been consigned to the dustbin of history, so this should all have been moot. When Paulson took Fannie and Freddie over, he told President George W. Bush in a meeting at the Oval Office, and he later told the whole country at a press conference, that this was a "time out" that should be used to

22   "permanently address the structural issues presented" by
      Fannie and Freddie, by which he meant their conflicting respon-
      sibilities to the mission of homeownership as well as to their
      bottom lines. Soon, the government, which had a longstand-
      ing love-hate relationship with the companies it had created,
      and a co-dependent one at that, would wind down and eventu-
      ally abolish them. Why couldn't purely private companies per-
      form most, if not all, of Fannie and Freddie's role of packaging
      up mortgages, just like Wall Street banks did in the run-up to
      the financial crisis? "This is an opportunity to get rid of institu-
      tions that shouldn't exist," said Paul Volcker, the revered former
      chairman of the Federal Reserve, in 2011. The official view is still
      that Fannie and Freddie shouldn't exist. President Obama said,
      in 2013, "I believe that our housing system should operate where
      there's a limited government role and private lending should be
      the backbone of the housing market."

      But here we are in 2015, and Fannie and Freddie are more im-
      portant than ever before. The Dodd-Frank Wall Street Reform
      and Consumer Protection Act, which is supposed to reshape the
      financial sector and which President Obama signed into law in
      the summer of 2010, quite deliberately did not deal with Fannie
      and Freddie. Nothing has happened since then, either. Fannie
      and Freddie remain wards of the government. As longtime
      housing analyst Laurie Goodman wrote in a 2014 paper, "The
      current state of the GSEs can best be summed up in a single
      word: limbo."

      Meanwhile, the mortgage market in the United States has
      effectively been nationalized. This is precisely the opposite of
      what President Obama said he wanted. According to Goodman,

from 2008 to 2013, the government was the major source of credit for most people who got mortgages, and the only source of credit for less-than-pristine borrowers. Goodman calculates that the government share of the home mortgage market was in the range of 78 to 85 percent, with Fannie and Freddie making up most of that. Compare that to the 20 years before the financial crisis, during which roughly half of all mortgages were financed without backing from the federal government, according to the Congressional Budget Office.

Nor have Fannie and Freddie shrunk. By some measures, they have gotten bigger. They still have some $5 trillion of securities outstanding. Foreign investors still own an estimated 15 to 20 percent of GSE securities. And by one important measure, Fannie and Freddie are in more precarious shape than they were in the run-up to the crisis. Because the government is taking practically every penny of profit that the two companies generate to shrink the federal deficit, Fannie and Freddie have not been allowed to rebuild any capital, which could absorb losses in the event of another downturn in the housing market. (By contrast, the government has forced the other big financial institutions to hold more capital than they did before 2008.) "We are faced with running this business with really no cushion. It is a challenging situation for us," Fannie Mae CEO Timothy Mayopoulos said on a conference call in early 2015.

"It's very scary to us personally," says Ryan Israel, who works for Pershing Square, one of the hedge funds that's suing the government. "It's the last unsolved issue of the financial crisis, and the ramifications are enormous for everyone."

Downfall

Part One

Subprime

"If you're not relevant, you're unprofitable, and you're not serving the mission."
—Dan Mudd, CEO of Fannie Mae, 2005–2008

The story of how Fannie and Freddie came to be put in conservatorship is one of petty personality conflicts, global political concerns, incompetent oversight, tremendously bad business decisions in the midst of a housing bubble the likes of which no one has ever seen before—and ultimately, the flawed model of Fannie and Freddie. There will probably never be a single version of the truth upon which everyone agrees. There are a number of people, including Tim Howard, chief financial officer of Fannie Mae from 1990 to 2004, and Franklin Raines, Fannie's chief executive officer from 1999 to 2004, who claim that if the experienced senior management teams of both companies hadn't been pushed out at precisely the most dangerous time in history—2004, just when the mortgage market was becoming dangerously overheated—it would all have been different. In Raines's view, Fannie and Freddie, which at the height of their power set and enforced the standards by which business was done, sat at the center of the housing finance world, holding it all together. "When the leadership of Fannie and Freddie were decapitated, it was like a pinwheel coming apart," says Raines.

It's certainly true that in the mid-2000s, Fannie and Freddie were in tatters. A major scandal over complicated allegations about Fannie and Freddie's accounting practices—over the charge, essentially, that Raines, Howard, and other executives had manipulated their companies' results to maximize their own compensation—led to a vast, distracting reworking of both companies and, indeed, the decapitation of the leadership. A Fannie executive says that because the process was so onerous—there were about 2,800 outside lawyers, accountants, and others hired to clean it up at a cost of over $1 billion—Fannie never again had the same top executive team for a full year. And as this person puts it, "It was a problem, not having a team that knew each other when the industry was going to hell."

It's also clearly true that the industry *was* going to hell, thanks to the explosion in subprime lending. Subprime lending had first taken off in the 1990s. The mortgages were sold to Wall Street, not to Fannie and Freddie. Instead of guaranteeing the homeowner's ability to pay, as Fannie and Freddie do, Wall Street paid the credit-rating agencies to assign ratings that were supposed to measure the risk of nonpayment. So-called private-label securities that were given triple A's—the safest possible rating—were supposed to be as safe as Fannie and

Freddie securities. Indeed, after much lobbying by the Federal
Reserve, banks, and investment banks, the international body
known as the Basel Committee, which assesses the riskiness
of various securities for purposes of determining how much
capital financial institutions must hold, ruled in 2001 that private-label securities rated triple-A and double-A were just as
safe as the corresponding GSE securities. "This action, as much
as any other, opened the floodgates to the reckless private label securitization of the most toxic mortgage products," noted
Josh Rosner, managing director at research consultancy Graham
Fisher, in a 2012 testimony to a congressional subcommittee.

Lending to people who couldn't afford traditional mortgages
was supposed to increase homeownership, which, of course, was
what politicians have long pushed for. But subprime lending
was never truly about homeownership. In the 1990s, much of
the business of the new breed of lenders was so-called cash-out
refinancings, in which a borrower would refinance her mortgage
into a bigger one, and take the difference in cash that could be
spent on bills, or on home improvements—really, on anything.
According to a 2000 joint study published by the Treasury and
the Department of Housing and Urban Development, by 1999 a
staggering 82 percent of subprime mortgages were refinancings;
and in nearly 60 percent of those cases, the borrower pulled out
cash, thereby adding to her debt burden. One could argue that
refinancing worked to undermine, not strengthen, homeownership, by generating a lot of overextended homeowners who
couldn't make their mortgage payments.

The first wave of subprime was too small to get most
people's attention. And at the end of the 1990s, many of the

28   subprime lenders crashed and burned amid proliferating con-
        sumer complaints about abusive lending practices and the dry-
        ing up of credit after the 1998 crisis in emerging economies. But
        within just a few years, subprime lending was back, and bigger
        than ever. An avalanche of companies was selling mortgage loans
        directly to Wall Street, bypassing Fannie and Freddie. Subprime
        mortgages rose from 8 percent of mortgage originations in 2003
        to 20 percent in 2005. So-called Alt-A mortgages—loans made
        to people with good credit who couldn't or wouldn't document
        their income, or with some other nontraditional feature, and
        thus considered more risky than "prime" loans and less risky
        than "subprime" loans—also exploded. By 2006, private-label
        issuance reached $1.15 trillion, and an astonishing 71 percent
        of the mortgages were either subprime or Alt-A, according to
        the Financial Crisis Inquiry Commission, which was tasked
        with investigating the causes of the 2008 crisis. According to
        analysis by Jason Thomas, now the director of research at the
        Carlyle Group, only about a third of subprime mortgages that
        were turned into securities between 2000 and 2007 were used
        to buy homes.
            Fannie and Freddie also benefited from the extraction of
        home equity. No one distinguished between a mortgage made
        to purchase a home and a refinancing, in part because no one
        foresaw the waves of refinancing that the falling interest rates
        of the 1990s and 2000s would bring. Between 2004 and 2007,
        homeowners cashed out approximately $966 billion in home
        equity from Freddie Mac–backed loans, according to a Govern-
        ment Accountability Office report. In 2006, cash-out refinances
        accounted for nearly 30 percent of all refinances at Freddie Mac.

Even so, as the private market boomed, Fannie and Freddie were rapidly becoming irrelevant. Their market share fell from 57 percent in 2003 to 42 percent in 2004 and to 37 percent in 2006, according to data gathered by the Financial Crisis Inquiry Commission. Why? The private market was leaving them behind. A 2005 internal presentation at Fannie Mae noted, with some alarm, "Private label volume surpassed Fannie Mae volume for the first time." As an executive from a major subprime lending company called New Century told Congress in early 2004, subprime lenders were necessary to the economy, because they provided credit to "customers who do not satisfy the stricter credit, documentation or other underwriting standards prescribed by Fannie Mae and Freddie Mac." He went on to point out that while over 40 percent of New Century's loans were made to borrowers who didn't have to verify their income, Fannie and Freddie "have more stringent income documentation guidelines." He also continued, "For refinance transactions, Fannie Mae and Freddie Mac do not generally permit a borrower to exceed a 90 percent loan-to-value ratio on a cash-out refinance loan. We and other nonprime lenders allow borrowers to take out more cash."

But even before Raines, Brendsel, and other top executives were forced out, Fannie and Freddie had embraced their enemy in a subterranean and deeply perverse way, and one that only mega-institutions with a dual mandate of making profits and satisfying a government mandate would have done. They began buying what were supposedly the safest part of Wall Street's private-label securities—those that were rated triple-A—as investments that they would own on their own balance sheets,

30   and they did so in huge volumes that only institutions of their size could handle. It was actually Freddie, which in most things followed Fannie, that dove into this business first, and bought much more. According to an Atlanta Federal Reserve working paper, Freddie and Fannie together purchased 3.8 percent of subprime issuance in 2001, 11.9 percent in 2002, 34.7 percent in 2003, 38.9 percent in 2004, and 28.9 percent in 2005, tapering to about 25 percent in 2006 and 2007. By the end of 2007, the two companies together held more than $313 billion in private-label mortgage-backed securities, according to a 2009 Government Accountability Office report. Most of it was owned by Freddie.

One reason Fannie and Freddie encouraged the very business that was threatening their existence was that the private-label mortgage-backed securities were, at first, profitable investments. Another reason was that they talked—or "conned," according to Judy Kennedy, the former president of the National Association of Affordable Housing Lenders—the Department of Housing and Urban Development into allowing these loans to count toward the congressionally mandated goals to provide affordable housing that Fannie and Freddie had had to meet since 1992. (Fannie initially didn't think these loans qualified for the goals, says one former employee, but soon began using them for the same reason.) Wall Street even began designing a special product just for Fannie and Freddie that was packed with loans that satisfied the goals.

But buying what would turn out to be Wall Street's fatally flawed securities wasn't the only bad decision Fannie and Freddie made. Dan Mudd, who replaced Franklin Raines as Fannie's CEO in 2005, was a Republican former Marine who had worked at General Electric before joining Fannie in 2000. He found himself under immense pressure to win back the market share Fannie was losing in the business of turning mortgages into securities. (It was a similar story over at Freddie Mac.) So both companies also began guaranteeing the risk that the homeowner won't pay—known as credit risk—on huge quantities of those risky Alt-A loans. In this, Fannie took the lead, purchasing a stunning $350 billion of these loans between 2005 and 2007, stamping them with its guarantee, and turning them into securities. In a presentation for a 2005 executive retreat, Tom Lund, who was then the head of Fannie's single-family business, put it this way: "We face two stark choices: stay the course [or] meet the market where the market is." According to an interview with staff of the Financial Crisis Inquiry Commission, Lund went on to say that if Fannie Mae stayed the course, it would maintain its credit discipline, protect the quality of its book, preserve capital, and be able to speak publicly about its concerns over the declining quality of mortgages. However, he said, Fannie would also face lower volumes and revenues, continued declines in market share, lower earnings, and a weakening of key customer relationships. It was simply a matter of relevance, Dan Mudd later told the FCIC. "If you're not relevant, you're unprofitable, and you're not serving the mission," he said. "And there was danger to profitability. I'm speaking more long term than in any given quarter or any given year. So this was a real strategic rethinking." "It was very interesting to me how market share—driven both Fannie and Freddie were," says a former executive. "It was how they measured themselves."

32   It wasn't done without trepidation. A former executive says that Lund, who complained that Fannie didn't have the capability or the infrastructure to deal with riskier mortgages, would sit in meetings shaking his head, saying, "I do not know how banks are pricing these." Lund also worried that by his calculations, as much as 35 percent of all home purchases were second homes, which indicated that widespread speculation was going on. In May 2005, he gave a speech to a mortgage industry group where he argued that the proliferation of nontraditional mortgage products had created risk layering, by which he meant loans that might combine, say, a very small down payment with a borrower who wouldn't document her income. (Even when Fannie began guaranteeing those massive quantities of risky Alt-A loans, the company tried to pick the best ones and avoid guaranteeing mortgages with layered risk.)

        We trust the regulators of the financial system to see problems and act to stop them. So why didn't the regulators put a stop to what was happening? During this period, an obscure federal agency, the Office of Federal Housing Enterprise Oversight (it was a casualty of the financial crisis and no longer exists), had responsibility for Fannie and Freddie. OFHEO understood that Fannie and Freddie were moving aggressively into the subprime mortgage market. Its March 2007 report noted that Fannie's new initiative to purchase higher-risk products included a plan to capture 20 percent of the subprime market by 2011. But OFHEO viewed this as a positive development, or at least as not alarming. Jim Lockhart, a Yale fraternity buddy of President George W. Bush's who had worked as the deputy commissioner of the Social Security Administration when there was much talk of privatizing Social Security, and who then became the chairman of OFHEO in 2006, later told the FCIC that there was so much focus on cleaning up the accounting and watching interest rate risk (changes in interest rates can cause big losses for those who own mortgages) that "credit risk was not emphasized as much as it should have been."

As for the Federal Reserve, which also has responsibility for the financial system, its powerful chairman from 1987 to 2006, Alan Greenspan, was long opposed to the power in the mortgage market that Fannie and Freddie wielded. Tim Howard, Fannie Mae's former CFO, would later charge that that was one reason no one tried to rein in the private market. "Following the lead of Fed chairman Alan Greenspan, [the Fed and the Treasury] actively were seeking to substitute free market principles, mechanisms and disciplines for government involvement and regulation wherever they could . . . subprime mortgages were the private market alternatives to loans financed by the GSEs," Howard wrote in a 2013 book titled *The Mortgage Wars: Inside Fannie Mae, Big-Money Politics, and the Collapse of the American Dream.* Later, many people would pat themselves on the back for identifying the GSEs as a disaster waiting to happen. But it's actually hard to find one person who identified the real cause of the problem. It was credit risk—the chance that home-owners won't be able to pay—and it would soon engulf the global financial system.

The Bazooka

"If you've got a bazooka, and people know you've got it, you may not have to take it out."
—Hank Paulson, Secretary of the Treasury, 2006–2009

In the summer of 2007, German Landesbanken—regional German banks—began to warn about losses due to heavy investments in U.S. private-label mortgage securities. Many would eventually need costly bailouts by the German government. Fannie and Freddie saw the trouble emerging in the mortgage markets—how could they not?—but they saw it as an opportunity not to pull back, but to win back the market share they had lost to Wall Street. "Our business model—investing in and guaranteeing mortgages—is a good one, so good that others want to 'take us out,'" stated Fannie Mae in its strategic plan for 2007 to 2011. By the end of August 2007, Fannie's stock, which had dropped to a low of $48 in the spring of 2005, was almost back to its 2004 peak of $70. By the first quarter of 2008, Fannie and Freddie were guaranteeing 80 percent of all U.S. mortgages, double their market share from two years earlier. As a result, Fannie and Freddie exploded in size, from $3.6 trillion in debt and mortgage-backed securities outstanding in 2006 to $4.9 trillion in 2007 and to $5.2 trillion in the summer of 2008. To back that up, they held just a comparative sliver of capital—$84 billion.

Few people saw that the bottom was about to fall out. Many politicians were pushing Fannie and Freddie to do more to support the softening housing market. "Some of us who have helped Fannie and Freddie in the past ought to jawbone them to do it," Chuck Schumer, the Democratic New York Senator, said. And even those who didn't like the GSEs saw that they needed them. Hank Paulson, who'd become Treasury Secretary in 2006, later told the FCIC that when he took office, he viewed Fannie and Freddie as a "disaster waiting to happen." He complained that foreign buyers didn't actually understand the two companies. "Try to go around the world and explain to one leader after another what this implicit-not-explicit government guarantee was about," he said, adding that he had to explain to leaders ranging from Angela Merkel of Germany to Nicolas Sarkozy of France to Hu Jintao of China that the United States government had no actual responsibility to pay off Fannie and Freddie's obligations, even though that assumption explained why many foreigners had viewed those obligations as safe investments. He said he told staffers that "the structure [of the companies] is so flawed that I don't want to leave Washington without there being some major attempt to make it better." But he also said that they were "the only game in town" once the housing market

36   dried up in the summer of 2007. Private capital, so plentiful in
the boom, simply disappeared. If a homeowner wanted a mortgage, it had to be one that could be sold to Fannie and Freddie.

The most striking moment came in the spring of 2008, just
after the dramatic rescue of Bear Stearns. At a press conference
on March 19, Paulson, Jim Lockhart, Dan Mudd, and Richard
Syron, the CEO of Freddie Mac, announced that the GSEs would
be permitted to reduce their capital in order to purchase or guarantee an additional $200 billion in mortgages. No one voiced
any public concern. "Fannie Mae and Freddie Mac are significant
participants in the mortgage market, and I am encouraged that
today's announcement will make more financing available in
this area," said Paulson. "The actions we're taking today make
the idea of a bailout nonsense in my mind," Lockhart said. "The
companies are safe and sound, and they will continue to be safe
and sound."

That was what he said in public. Privately, Lockhart wasn't
happy. "The idea strikes me as perverse, and I assume it would
seem perverse to the markets that a regulator would agree to
allow a regulatee to increase its very high mortgage credit risk
leverage (not to mention increasing interest rate risk) without
any new capital," he wrote in an e-mail to Mudd and Syron. "We
seem to have gone from 2 to 1 right through 1 to 1 to now 0 to 1."
Years later, in a presentation at the Milken Institute on the state
of mortgage finance, Lockhart said, "Frankly, regulators are subject to political pressure and that is part of the problem."

At the same time that the government was publicly reassuring investors, officials were pressuring the GSEs to raise more
capital. Between the start of 2007 and the summer of 2008,

Fannie and Freddie sold a combined $22 billion in so-called pre-
ferred stock, bringing their total outstanding preferred stock to
$34 billion. (Preferred stock pays a dividend like a bond.) The
buyers, at least initially, were individual investors in search of
dividends and community banks, who were encouraged to hold
GSE securities to bolster their own capital. This preferred stock,
ironically enough, would turn out to be a huge problem for the
government.

On March 10, *Barron's* ran a story titled "Is Fannie Mae the
Next Government Bailout?" The story noted Fannie's burgeoning losses, questioned its accounting, particularly on the huge
quantities of Alt-A and subprime mortgages, and noted that its
capital—its ability to cover its losses—was less than met the
eye. That was because a chunk of Fannie's supposed capital consisted of what are known as deferred tax assets—essentially,
rights to avoid paying taxes on profits in the future. (And if there
are no profits, then the ability to avoid taxes doesn't get you
very far.) The article concluded: "Just maybe a bailout of Fannie,
in effect a nationalization, would be a good thing. A retooled
Fannie could pursue its important social mission without the
distraction of trying to please Wall Street."

The analysis was very similar to that in a paper called
"Fannie Mae Insolvency and Its Consequences" that was circu-
lating among senior officials at the National Economic Council
and the Treasury. Even the language was similar. "A government
seizure is inevitable," it began. It noted the same accounting
concerns, and even ended with a version of the same conclusion: "A fully government owned guarantor of mortgage debt
might be exactly what is called for given the current housing

38   crisis . . . without the need to satisfy a fiduciary duty to shareholders, Fannie might finally be able to perform its affordable
housing mission in a helpful and proactive manner."

The Monday after the *Barron's* story ran, Fannie's stock fell
13 percent.

Then, in mid-July, stories appeared in both the *Wall Street
Journal* and the *New York Times*. The *Times* wrote: "Senior Bush
administration officials are considering a plan to have the government take over one or both of the companies and place them
in a conservatorship if their problems worsen." Fannie's stock
dropped 50 percent in two days. Any shareholder who thought
the government was going to take over the companies sold his
or her stake immediately. (Paulson has always said that neither
he nor anyone at the White House knew anything about a conservatorship strategy at that time.)

By the end of the month, Fannie's and Freddie's stock prices
were still falling, and it was becoming more difficult for them to
raise the debt they needed to buy mortgages. On July 30, with a
big push from Paulson, Congress passed a bill called the Housing
and Economic Recovery Act. HERA created a new, much stronger regulator for Fannie and Freddie, and for the Federal Home
Loan Banks. This new agency, the Federal Housing Finance
Agency, or FHFA, had the power, far too belatedly, to increase the
amount of capital Fannie and Freddie were required to hold. The
new law also temporarily gave the U.S. Treasury the ability to put
an unlimited amount of funds into the two companies. They could
do that via an existing mechanism known as "conservatorship,"
in which the companies would be taken over and nurtured back
to health, or via a new mechanism that critics had long sought

called receivership, which is a bit like bankruptcy, in which case
the losses were supposed to be apportioned out to creditors.

Paulson said he never intended to use the ability to put tax-payer money into Fannie and Freddie. "If you've got a bazooka, and people know you've got it, you may not have to take it out," Paulson explained to Congress. But in the view of many investors, the very ability of the government to step in made the need to do so inevitable. "When Paulson said he wouldn't use his ba-zooka, I read it to the contrary," one major investor in mortgages says. "Anyone in harm's way should run for the hills."

By the end of August, the shares of Fannie and Freddie had fallen some 85 percent in just eight months. Yu Yongding, who had served on the Monetary Policy Committee of the People's Bank of China, the country's central bank, told *Bloomberg*: "If the U.S. government allows Fannie and Freddie to fail and inter-national investors are not compensated adequately, the conse-quences will be catastrophic. If it is not the end of the world, it is the end of the current international financial system."

Paulson would later say that he figured out the government would have to take over Fannie and Freddie by mid-August; and so, inside the Treasury, frantic preparations were getting un-der way. Part of the problem was that, as the crisis intensified, regulators had continued to give both Fannie and Freddie what amounted to a clean bill of health; on August 22, the new regu-lator, FHFA, even sent both companies letters saying they were "adequately capitalized." As Paulson later wrote, "It would be suicide if we attempted to take control of Fannie and Freddie and they went to court only to have it emerge that the FHFA had said, in effect, that there were no problems."

So Paulson also wrote that his team "work[ed] hard to con-
vince FHFA to take a much more realistic view" of the issues
facing Fannie and Freddie, and brought in the investment bank
Morgan Stanley, as well as examiners from the Federal Reserve
and the Office of the Comptroller of the Currency. They concluded that Fannie and Freddie weren't so healthy after all. Both
GSEs were overstating their capital levels, because they were
underestimating how much they would lose on bad mortgages,
and because their deferred tax assets were worthless.

On September 4, FHFA sent both companies extremely
harsh mid-year review letters. That same day, Paulson met with
President Bush to tell him he was planning to take over Fannie
and Freddie. "Do they know it's coming, Hank?" President
Bush asked, according to Paulson's book. "'Mr. President,' I
said, 'We're going to move quickly and take them by surprise.
The first sound they'll hear is their heads hitting the floor.'"
On September 5, Paulson, Lockhart, and Fed chairman Ben
Bernanke met with the companies' CEOs and directors to tell
them they had no choice but to agree to conservatorship. The
management teams were told to go, and both Fannie and Freddie
had to immediately fire all their lobbyists. Paulson later called
the decision to take over Fannie and Freddie the "most impactful and the gutsiest thing we did."

The terms were, by design, both complicated and punitive. The government got the right to take 79.9 percent of the
common stock of both companies. Why not just national-
ize them and take 100 percent? "If the U.S. government were
to own more than 80 percent of either enterprise, there was a
sizable risk that the enterprises would be forced to consolidate

onto the government's balance sheet," explained analyst Laurie Goodman—meaning that the federal government's debt could skyrocket. Although the Treasury would provide very little up-front cash, it committed to putting in a great deal of money—up to $200 billion—as needed over time. Fannie and Freddie would have to pay a 10 percent interest rate on any funds the government advanced. Any money the Treasury put in would become senior preferred stock, which would have to be paid before any investor in either the preferred stock that had just been sold, or the GSEs' common shares, got anything.

The government funding assured the holders of Fannie and Freddie debt and mortgage-backed securities that they didn't have to worry about any losses: The U.S. government was standing behind them. But the dividend on the preferred stock that had just been sold was suspended—investors in the last batch, which was sold in May 2008, had barely gotten any payments at all. Although both the preferred stock and the common stock continued to trade on exchanges, due to the terms of the deal, it looked like any value that was left would all go to the government. Both the common stock and the existing preferred shares plunged to pennies. A member of the group that sets federal accounting guidelines later explained that government wasn't actually going to exercise its right to take ownership of Fannie and Freddie. Instead, the bailout was designed this way because "driving the stock market value to zero" would "prevent current shareholder speculation resulting in speculators taking advantage of government intervention at the expense of others," according to minutes of the meeting that became public in 2015.

42   The terms, of course, were radically less generous than what the government would soon do for big banks, which were given low-cost guarantees of their debt and capital infusions at a 5 percent interest rate instead of the 10 percent charged to Fannie and Freddie. In addition, the management teams of the banks that took government money weren't forced out. Overall, it's hard to find any consistency in the government's treatment of different companies in the crisis; there is also an argument that the banks needed kid-glove treatment because government policy toward one bank would have reverberations for all banks, whereas Fannie and Freddie, along with AIG, were unique. But there is also a contingent that believes what Tim Howard would later contend, which is that it is difficult to "conclude anything other than that Treasury took advantage of the 2008 financial crisis to advance their long-held policy objective of removing [Fannie and Freddie] as the centerpieces of the U.S. mortgage finance system."

But Howard's contention also raises a question: If the government wanted to get rid of the two companies, why did it use government's powers to save them? The answer is that the government couldn't afford to let Fannie and Freddie go—and it still can't.

One reason was sheer necessity. When the crisis hit, private capital did what private capital does: It completely deserted an asset class it no longer liked. There was absolutely no capital available to finance mortgages—and if the mortgage market shut down, the economy would shut down with it. Fannie and Freddie were all that was left. "They have to be used to keep the flow of capital going to the housing market," Larry Summers, who became the head of the National Economic Council under President Obama, said in 2008. And if they were kept alive and under the government's thumb, they could be used to support the mortgage market, without interference from shareholders, who after all had been reduced to almost nothing.

Another reason was what China's Yu Yongding had warned about. Foreign institutions, mainly central banks, owned around $1 trillion of agency debt and mortgage-backed securities, according to a paper by New York Federal Reserve economists. The Chinese and Japanese between them owned most of this. If Paulson and his team had created any doubt about the safety of Fannie and Freddie's debt or their ability to stand behind the mortgage-backed securities they had guaranteed, it would have instantly thrown into doubt how much of their money these creditors would get. On top of that, China and Japan also owned almost half of the U.S. Treasury debt in foreign hands at the time. "A default on these [GSE] securities would likely have had significant international political ramifications," according to the Federal Reserve paper. "There was a risk that allowing a default on these securities would raise questions about the creditworthiness of the U.S. government." Of course, the last thing anyone ever wants, but particularly in a moment of crisis, is a loss of confidence in U.S. sovereign debt.

Fannie and Freddie's debt was laced throughout the U.S. banking system, with U.S. banks also owning over a trillion dollars in GSE securities. And Fannie and Freddie had major derivative contracts with all the big Wall Street firms. The implosion of those contracts could have thrown another huge kink into the system. "Letting Fannie and Freddie fail would have taken down

44   the whole financial system," Paulson says. "It would have been worse than the Great Depression."

In other words, for all the desire to impose losses on creditors via receivership, it would turn out that no one was willing to pull the trigger in a time of crisis. Paulson would later say that as long as U.S. government was extending a line of credit, receivership versus conservatorship was a "distinction without a difference," because under either structure, the government would have ensured that creditors and investors in Fannie and Freddie's securities didn't have to worry about the safety of their money, and with government backing, the companies would have continued to function much as they always did. But receivership would have been a spookier word at a very fragile time. It also contained provisions that were supposed to force a fairly swift decision as to the ultimate resolution of the GSEs. Conservatorship was probably a more stabilizing solution—but it was never supposed to be permanent. Instead, conservatorship deferred the political battle over the fate of Fannie and Freddie to a time when we weren't in crisis—or at least that was the idea. Paulson explained to President Bush that he chose what he called a "time out" to avoid a "holy war." "I was keen to avoid any existential debate on the two companies that might bog down in partisan politics on the Hill," he later wrote. Senator Schumer said, upon the announcement of conservatorship: "This plan will be met with broad acceptance in Congress, because it doesn't prejudge the ultimate fate of Fannie Mae and Freddie Mac." "We wanted to force Congress to make a decision," says another person who was part of the conservatorship decision. "I agreed at the time, but we have learned the pitfalls."

Dan Mudd would later tell the FCIC that he disagreed with conservatorship in part because "the government could not enunciate a clear rationale for the takeover, had no specific plan for running the company in conservatorship, and could not point to any instance where the company had failed to meet a government request."

Certainly, no one who was involved would have guessed that seven years later, the GSEs would still be in the state of limbo known as conservatorship.

The Blame Game

"The root cause of the financial crisis was not deregulation, but dumb regulation."
—Jeb Hensarling, Chairman of the House Financial Services Committee

Even in the fall of 2008, the worst of the financial crisis, a narrative began to gain currency with astonishing speed: The crisis was all Fannie and Freddie's fault. As John McCain, then the Republican candidate for president, put it in a stump speech, Fannie and Freddie were "the match that started this forest fire."

This story line would soon expand. It wasn't just that Fannie and Freddie were responsible for the crisis, but that the genesis of the problem—the original sin—was Congress's 1992 imposition on Fannie and Freddie of affordable-housing goals, which required the GSEs to guarantee certain numbers of mortgages made to lower-income borrowers. In this view, Fannie and

Freddie bulked up on risky mortgages, starting not in the 2000s, but rather in the 1990s, for one reason and one reason only: to satisfy congressionally mandated goals to provide affordable housing.

There is a lot at stake in this debate. If you can place the blame for the crisis of 2008 in its entirety on the government, then you can absolve the private market and Wall Street of any guilt. The idea that the pure and free market solves all problems—what Fannie's former CEO Franklin Raines calls "marketification"—is still as beautiful as ever. You can then argue that no new regulations are needed—the only fix is to never again have any policies that help poor people buy homes. And, of course, to get the government entirely out of the housing market. In a recent congressional hearing, Jeb Hensarling, the conservative Republican chairman of the House Financial Services Committee, said, "The root cause of the financial crisis was not deregulation, but dumb regulation; regulations and statutes that either incented or mandated financial institutions to loan money to people to buy homes they ultimately could not afford to keep."

Several of the most vocal proponents of this idea are conservative economist and former Reagan White House counsel Peter Wallison, and Ed Pinto, a former chief credit officer of Fannie Mae who left the company in the late 1980s. Both men now work at the conservative think tank American Enterprise Institute.

The key to the claim is Pinto's research, which he says shows that by June 2008, 31 million mortgages, or over half of the total in the United States, were subprime or otherwise high-risk

48   ones, and that most of them were on the books of government
agencies, mainly Fannie and Freddie.

In Wallison's 2015 book, *Hidden in Plain Sight*, which also
leans on Pinto's numbers, he argues that it was not the private sector that first pushed into subprime lending, but rather
Fannie and Freddie that began to guarantee riskier and riskier
mortgages in the 1990s in order to meet their affordable-
housing goals. According to Wallison, the regulators didn't
see this—the world didn't see this—because Fannie and
Freddie didn't clearly disclose the horrendously risky loans
they were guaranteeing. Because they dominated the market,
their reduced standards inevitably spread to the private sector. He says it was the failure of these riskier "non traditional"
loans, which were mainly on the books of government agencies,
that caused housing prices to fall, thereby sparking losses in
the private sector. Wallison concludes that the private sector
was a "minor factor compared to the role of the government's
housing policies."

Wallison served as one of the ten commissioners of the
Financial Crisis Inquiry Commission, but he did not sign off on
the majority report, which was critical of Fannie and Freddie but
assigned little blame to the housing goals. In his 95-page dissent, he claimed that the Democratic-majority FCIC essentially
ignored Pinto's research due to its own political inclinations,
which were to blame the private sector. "Any objective investigation of the causes of the financial crisis would have looked
carefully at Ed Pinto's research, exposed it to the members of
the Commission, taken Pinto's testimony, and tested the accu-
racy of Pinto's research," he wrote. "But the Commission took

none of these steps. Pinto's research was never made available
to the other members of the FCIC."

While the three other Republican commissioners on the
FCIC did not sign off on the majority report, they also didn't
sign on to Wallison's view. They wrote their own dissent, in
which they found that "poorly designed government housing
policies" distorted the market, but that "single cause explanations" were "too simplistic." E-mails exchanged by the other
three Republican commissioners and their staffs show that
they thought Wallison was going overboard. For example, one
Republican commissioner, Douglas Holtz-Eakin, who served as
the director of the Congressional Budget Office under President
George W. Bush, sent an e-mail to the commission's vice chairman, Bill Thomas, the longtime Republican representative from
California, stating: "I continue to think that Peter overplays
the mortgage issue," according to a report investigating the attacks on the FCIC which was done in 2011 by the Democratic
staff of the House Committee on Oversight and Government
Reform. In one exchange, Thomas's special assistant referred
to Wallison as "intractable" and wrote: "Everyone agrees that
there is simply no way to make Peter happy." Later, a colleague
at Thomas's law firm wrote: "I think wmt [William M. Thomas]
is going to push to find out if pinto is being paid by anyone."
(Wallison says today that he "came to the conclusion that my
fellow Republican commissioners did not want to blame George
Bush's policies for the crisis, so [like the Democrats] focused
solely on the private sector.")

There is truth to the broad argument that government
housing policies, of which the GSEs were one instrument,

50   helped cause the crisis. The government did push for weaker
      lending standards, and Fannie and Freddie certainly helped fa-
      cilitate that. And there is an argument that Fannie and Freddie
      helped blow the bubble bigger than it otherwise would have
      been, by guaranteeing Alt-A mortgages just as the market was
      peaking, and early on, by purchasing such large quantities of
      Wall Street's private-label securities for their portfolios. Some
      Wall Streeters argue that in the early years of the bubble, absent
      Fannie's and Freddie's demands for the securities, the Street
      wouldn't have been able to find buyers for all of its private-
      label product, which by definition would have limited the size
      of the market.

      It is also clear that over time, as the affordable-housing
      goals were ratcheted upwards, especially in the Bush
      Administration—which had its own reasons for doing so—
      meeting them became much more difficult and required Fannie
      and Freddie to do business they otherwise would not have done.
      Says a former Fannie executive, "I think the housing goals were
      really important in the early 1990s. Until then, we had no data,
      and the whole regime forced us to pay attention. But late in the
      game, the goals were ratcheted up to limits that were unrealistic."

      But Wallison's narrative can't be close to the entirety of
      the story. There is a big difference between a 30-year fixed-
      rate fully documented mortgage offered to a less creditworthy
      customer—which is the sort of riskier mortgage Fannie and
      Freddie mostly did in the 1990s—and the reckless loans that
      proliferated in the bubble, like adjustable-rate zero–down-
      payment mortgages where the borrower simply states his
      or her income; nor does the existence of the first type of loan

automatically presage the second. Fannie and Freddie's market share of mortgages that were turned into securities plunged as the second sort of mortgage took off. By the later, most dangerous years of the bubble they were not even the dominant buyers of risky private-label securities. David Fiderer, a former banker turned journalist, calculates that from 2005 to 2007, roughly $2.9 trillion of private-label first-lien single-family mortgage securities were issued, only about 15 percent of which were purchased by Fannie and Freddie, and they bought the safest possible part. That supposedly safer part of the securities— the triple-A-rated ones—became increasingly easy to sell because so many buyers around the world were looking for "safe" investments. As for the riskier pieces, it was a Wall Street invention—the collateralized debt obligation—that became the buyer. Without them, the last frenzied years of the bubble wouldn't have been possible.

The narrative that blames Fannie and Freddie and the affordable-housing goals ignores some other inconvenient facts. Among them:

- The first wave of subprime lenders in the 1990s grew up outside the GSEs. The survivors from these companies became the dominant subprime lenders in the second wave, after 2000. The men who ran these companies were entrepreneurs who saw a chance to make money, not supplicants trying to please Congress.
- By law, Fannie and Freddie were required to have mortgage insurance on any loan with a greater than 80 percent loan-to-value ratio. The mortgage insurers were purely private

companies. As Fiderer has pointed out, absent the private sector's willingness to take the risk on these high loan-to-value mortgages, Fannie and Freddie wouldn't have been able to insure those loans.

- The financial crisis that peaked in 2008 didn't begin with tremors at Fannie and Freddie. Instead, one of the earliest cracks came with the German Landesbanken, which needed bailouts thanks to losses from private-sector loans. New Century and other major subprime lenders were bankrupt before either Fannie or Freddie even reported a quarterly loss, making it awfully hard to argue that a loss of confidence in mortgages guaranteed by the GSEs was what brought these companies down.

- Because Fannie and Freddie themselves took the losses on all of the securities they backed or owned, none of the losses that brought down AIG and Lehman Brothers and almost brought down the rest of the financial system were caused by GSE-guaranteed loans.

It's also too simplistic to place all the blame for what Fannie and Freddie did do on the affordable-housing goals. All but two of the dozens of current and former Fannie Mae employees and regulators interviewed by the FCIC said that reaching the goals was not the primary driver of Fannie's move into risky lending. (The two who blamed the goals were Pinto and another man who left Fannie in the early 1990s.) Alt-A loans, a big part of Fannie and Freddie's problems, mostly didn't qualify for the goals. Many of the goals were based on borrowers' income levels, and Alt-A loans often had undocumented income. David Min, a former congressional staffer who is now an assistant professor of law at the University of California, Irvine, did his own analysis of Pinto's numbers, and found that roughly 65 percent of the "high-risk" loans that Pinto attributed to the affordable-housing goals were actually ineligible for the goals. When a Republican member of the FCIC pressed Ken Bacon, a former Fannie Mae executive, as to why Fannie began to move into higher-risk loans, Bacon responded: "It's very hard to any one person to sit as the market moves and say 'I'm smarter than everyone in this market.' Everyone was getting into the market, and I just can't give you a breaking point. Over time, we started doing things we used not to do."

In addition to disregarding what former GSE executives say, Wallison also ignores the internal Fannie and Freddie presentations made public by the FCIC that show them debating their move into riskier loans in the mid-2000s. If, as he argues, Fannie and Freddie were in the subprime business all along, it's hard to come up with a good explanation for the document trail that chronicles the internal angst.

Nor do Wallison and Pinto's numbers reconcile well with observed reality. Fiderer asked a simple question: If there were really 31 million "risky" mortgages, and Fannie and Freddie were responsible for half of them, why was the peak rate of serious delinquency for GSE-backed loans only about 1.8 million? The reason is that Pinto defines "risk" far differently than most and includes a large number of loans that, measured by loss rates, didn't turn out to be particularly risky. Another reality check is that if Fannie and Freddie led the race to the bottom, then you would expect to see much higher loss rates on their loans.

Instead, the opposite is true. The FCIC researchers ended up rejecting Pinto's analysis because they found that the loss rates on the GSEs' loans were actually far smaller than those on comparable private-sector loans. But they did meet with him multiple times, and produced two detailed memos about mortgage performance, one of which was a direct response to his analysis. These, along with Pinto's original analysis, were sent to all the commissioners; Wallison even forwarded Pinto's response to one memo to the commissioners himself. There is also a two-hour-long videotaped interview with Pinto. All of this documentation is available online at the FCIC archives at Stanford University. "No matter what the facts say, Peter Wallison will continue to assert his claims that Elvis is alive and that the earth revolves around the sun," says Phil Angelides, the California Democrat who chaired the FCIC. "I understand it's a very deliberate effort to redirect the focus and the blame," he continues, "but I'm struck by the sloppiness and the outright fabrications."

Yet another way to measure Fannie and Freddie's contribution to the crisis is by looking at their share of actual cash losses. Mark Zandi, the chief economist at Moody's, points out that at the end of 2013, approximately $1 trillion in credit losses on pre-crisis loans had been realized. The best performers were Fannie and Freddie, with a realized loss rate of 2.7 percent. Then came depository institutions, like banks, which had a realized loss rate of 5.8 percent. The strong outlier was private-label mortgage securities, with a realized loss rate of 23 percent, seven times that of the GSEs.

Neither Pinto nor Wallison denies these loss figures. In his book, Wallison writes, "There is no question that the [risky

mortgages] acquired by the GSEs . . . were of better quality than
the loans that private sector was securitizing." One explanation,
he argues, is that Fannie and Freddie "drove the private issuers
further out on the risk curve." As for Pinto, he wrote in one of his
memos to the FCIC that "as Fannie and Freddie began to poach
increasingly on Wall Street's turf, Wall Street had a choice—to
abandon the subprime business entirely, or to move further out
on the risk curve in order to maintain their business."

Saying that the government's gigantic footprint pushed
the private sector to the fringes of the market, where the ugli-
est loans that caused the lion's share of the losses were, is a very
different and far more nuanced argument than saying that bad
loans held by government entities due to affordable-housing
requirements were the primary cause of the crisis. And this
version leaves a lot of other factors unexplained. Among them:
Why was there so much money, for a period of time, to be made
on those fringes? Why didn't the private sector do what it was
supposed to do best, namely manage risk?

In the end, one lesson is that when you mix together the
government and the private market, they interact in ways that
are hard to predict in advance and difficult to untangle even after
the fact.

But there's another lesson too, which both the pro-GSE
and the anti-GSE narratives ignore. The majority of risky mortgages were not made to put people in homes. Rather, they were
cash-out refinancings and purchases of investment properties.
And there's some additional research that suggests that putting poor people in homes was not the source of the problem. A
study published by the National Bureau of Economic Research

56   in early 2014 says that the wealthiest 40 percent of borrowers got 55 percent of the new loans in 2006—the peak year of the bubble—and over the next three years, they were responsible for nearly 60 percent of delinquencies.

In other words, the crisis doesn't tell us much, if anything, about whether policies to help people buy homes are a good or a bad idea. What the crisis proves is that the crazed extension of credit to borrowers at any income level is a really bad idea.

But in Washington, it's far from clear that the real lessons matter. "I wish it was simply a matter of telling the truth," says John Taylor, the president of the National Community Reinvestment Coalition. "This is a political issue. It means you don't have to rely on facts. You can make up your own." At least in one sense, Wallison has already won, because for a long time, it was hard to find a Fannie or Freddie friend, even among the Democrats. As a former Fannie executive says, "The GSEs had a reputation for being Democratic organizations, but most Democrats ran from supporting them too." "People have a visceral reaction to them," marvels one longtime mortgage investor. "People want to say, 'I killed them.'"

Origins

Part Two

Housing Industrial Complex

"What's good for American housing is good for Fannie Mae."
   —Jim Johnson, CEO of Fannie Mae, 1991–1998

Fannie Mae and Freddie Mac aren't dead. But they're not really alive either—they're zombie agencies, still mired in a conservatorship that was supposed to be temporary, the last major financial institutions to remain in post-crisis uncertainty.
Although, unlike the other institutions that went down in the
crisis, they have a mandated social mission to fulfill, in the eyes
of critics they aren't fulfilling it—they aren't in good enough
shape financially to back anything but ultra-safe mortgages.
Conversely, they are so undercapitalized that they have not yet
left the realm of posing global systemic risk. They have managed to achieve a worst-of-both-worlds status: too political to
be financially secure, but too financially insecure to accomplish
their political mission. They have become a deficit-reduction

device for the federal government, which may help in the short
run but can't be sustained in the long run. Or as Jim Parrott,
a senior advisor with the National Economic Council in the
Obama Administration and now a senior fellow at the Urban
Institute, wrote in a recent brief, the current system "attracts
too little private capital, provides too little mortgage credit, and
still poses too much risk to the taxpayer." It is now probably too
late in his term for President Obama to solve the problem. His
successor will almost certainly have to.

It's impossible to understand why Fannie and Freddie are
such a difficult problem to solve without going back long before
the financial crisis—to a time when Fannie and Freddie were
two of the wealthiest, most powerful companies around.

On a sunny Monday in June 2002, President George W.
Bush stood in the St. Paul African Methodist Episcopal Church,
in a gentrifying neighborhood on the south side of Atlanta. In
the audience, in prime seats, were Franklin Raines, the CEO of
Fannie Mae from 1999 to 2004, and Leland Brendsel, the CEO
of Freddie Mac from 1987 to 2003. President Bush was there to
unveil an initiative aimed at helping 5.5 million minority families buy homes before the end of the decade. "Part of being a secure America," he said, "is to encourage homeownership." After
the event, Brendsel and Raines flew back to Washington on Air
Force One.

This scene was emblematic of what Ed DeMarco, an economist who would later oversee Fannie and Freddie as the acting
head of the agency that regulates them, and others came to de-
scribe as the housing industrial complex. It was (and is) an extremely effective, incredibly durable, and debatably unhealthy

60   alliance between politicians, private industry, not-for-profit community organizations, Fannie and Freddie, and others who have a stake in the enormous enterprise that is the American mortgage market.

For many years, Fannie Mae and Freddie Mac, but particularly Fannie, sat at the epicenter of that complex. Jim Johnson, the Washington power broker—the *Washington Post* once called him "the chairman of the universe"—who served as Fannie's CEO from 1991 to 1998, used to paraphrase an old motto about General Motors this way: "What's good for American housing is good for Fannie Mae." It's Johnson who is usually credited with building the formidable political machine that Fannie became.

One of the engines of Fannie's political power was its practice of donating money to politically plugged-in housing not-for-profits that supported its agenda. Fannie also used its stock—$350 million worth—to seed its own Fannie Mae Foundation. Over time, the foundation gave away hundreds of millions to organizations ranging from the Congressional Black Caucus to the Cold Climate Housing Research Center in Fairbanks, Alaska. The money was the basis for countless photo ops for politicians, who could showcase all the good they were doing for their communities. And it meant that Fannie had politicians around the country, from mayors to senators, whom it could call upon if it needed help.

Another engine was the way Fannie hired. "Every congressional staffer who had any connection to housing knew they had a job with Fannie when they left," says one longtime Washingtonian. The *Washington Monthly* once declared that after Bill Clinton left the White House, he should go to Fannie because "scoring an executive post at Fannie Mae is recognized around establishment Washington as the equivalent of winning the lottery." That it was.

The list of those who worked for or lobbied for Fannie or Freddie is a who's who of Washington: Robert Zoellick, who was President George W. Bush's deputy secretary of state and then the president of the World Bank. Tom Donilon, who was Obama's national security advisor. Jamie Gorelick, who was the deputy attorney general in the Clinton Administration, and Arne Christensen, who was the chief of staff to Newt Gingrich, the former House majority leader. Chicago mayor Rahm Emanuel served on Freddie's board. Right-wing godfather Grover Norquist lobbied for Fannie. Newt Gingrich was a consultant for Freddie, and Ralph Reed was a consultant for Fannie. Ron Klain, who became the Ebola czar under Obama, lobbied for Fannie. It goes on and on.

Not surprisingly, Fannie Mae had a reputation for never losing a fight. "The old political reality was that we always won, we took no prisoners, and we faced little organized political opposition" is how Dan Mudd, Fannie's last real CEO, later criticized the agency's golden years. "Fannie has this grandmotherly image, but they will castrate you, decapitate you, tie you up, and throw you in the Potomac," a congressional source told the magazine *International Economy* in the late 1990s. "They are absolutely ruthless."

This was not what was envisioned when Fannie Mae was created in 1938 during Franklin Roosevelt's presidency, toward the end of the Great Depression.

Up until the 1930s, homeownership may have been part of the rhetoric of American politicians, but worrying about how people would finance those purchases wasn't part of the deal. This system didn't work very well. There were devastating examples of housing speculation gone wrong throughout the preceding century, including stories of speculators luring naïve families to frontier lands with grandiose promises that stripped away life savings, according to academic Sarah Lehman Quinn's dissertation "Government Policy, Housing, and the Origins of Securitization, 17880–1968." Between 1800 and 1820, the government did get involved by setting up offices that provided credit for land purchases; widespread defaults forced Congress to forgive many of these debts. "Capitalists, both real and fictitious, have engaged extensively in this business [of land speculation]," wrote one critic at the time. "The banks have conspired with the government to promote it; the former by lending money to the speculator, the latter by its wretched system of selling land on credit." At the end of that century, there was a national housing crash after a so-called farm mortgage craze in which mortgage brokers and nationally organized savings and loans, or thrifts, promised investors on the East Coast, and even abroad, high returns on the Western frontier. Drought and deflation derailed that. By the 1920s, mortgages were typically three to ten years in length, and required high down payments, as much as 50 percent. Homeowners often only paid interest, not principal, so the mortgage had to be repaid or refinanced at maturity in one big "balloon" or "bullet" payment. And there was huge variability in mortgage rates based on whether someone lived on the East Coast, where more lenders were based, or

West Coast, where a borrower might pay double the rate. But the Depression, which set off a vicious circle of plunging home prices and lack of access to credit, made a historically bad situation seem completely untenable. By the peak of the Depression, the national delinquency rate was 50 percent, according to Professor David Min, and lenders—primarily mutually owned building-and-loan societies—were failing in large numbers.

Homeownership was of course part of Roosevelt's rhetoric. "A nation of homeowners, of people who own a real share in their land, is unconquerable," he said. But housing to him was mainly an indispensable part of a broader economic approach. In the spring of 1932, when he was governor of New York and a presidential candidate, he gave a radio address. "Roosevelt Charges Federal Neglect of 'Little Fellow,'" was the *New York Times* headline. "These unhappy times call for the building of plans that rest upon the forgotten, the unorganized but the indispensable units of economic power, for plans . . . that build from the bottom up and not from the top down, that put their faith once more in the forgotten man at the bottom of the economic pyramid," he said.

Later, in a 1936 speech to the National Association of Real Estate Boards—which would become the politically powerful National Association of Realtors—Roosevelt said, "We have not yet found a satisfactory solution to one of the most fundamental of our economic problems—the provision for all American citizens of the kind of homes in which they have a right to live. I know you, with me, will not be content until a sound housing program is established for the whole nation."

The attempts to fix the housing crisis brought about by the Depression, which became the roots of the housing finance system we have today, actually began with President Herbert Hoover. In the summer of 1932, Congress passed the Federal Home Loan Bank Act; the idea was that federally backed regional banks would make cash advances to their local member banks, thereby encouraging those banks to lend. After Roosevelt took office in 1933, Congress passed the National Housing Act, which created the Federal Housing Administration. The FHA offered to insure lenders against defaults on long-term mortgages with low down payments. It was meant to calm everything down by encouraging lenders to lend—after all, the government bore the credit risk—and borrowers to borrow, by offering them certainty about the interest they would owe, and a long time to pay back the money. In 1936, the FHA reported to Congress that "the long term amortized mortgage has gained nation-wide acceptance at uniform lower interest rates in all sections of the United States."

The National Housing Act also included a provision that created privately owned national mortgage associations that would buy the new FHA-insured mortgages from lenders. It wasn't enough for lenders not to have to worry about borrowers defaulting. If they also knew that they could instantly turn their loans into cash, they'd be even more willing to lend. The associations were supposed to be funded by private capital; as Roosevelt told the nation's realtors, "I feel strongly that it is a part of your responsibility to help us discover the ways in which private capital can cooperate with public authorities in improving the housing conditions of the nation as a whole."

But in the three years after the new associations were authorized, none were set up. So to demonstrate proof of concept, in 1938, the FHA helped set up a government-owned entity to buy the loans it guaranteed. This entity soon became known as the Federal National Mortgage Association, or FNMA—or Fannie Mae. Jesse Jones, then the chairman of the Reconstruction Finance Corporation (which was set up by Hoover to lend money to companies and local governments in the Depression) told the *New York Times* that if private companies wanted to set up similar organizations in various cities, the RFC would match them dollar for dollar. None were ever set up.

Maybe the private sector didn't want to compete with the government, or maybe, bruised and battered from the Depression, it didn't want anything to do with mortgage risk. Maybe both were the case. But certainly the mortgage market in the United States developed differently than it would have, and differently from other countries', at least in part as a result of the government's involvement. In its sponsorship of a congressionally chartered company to buy up mortgages, the U.S. was, and is, unique. In much of the world, mortgages are financed either via bank deposits, or via what are known as covered bonds, in which banks issue bonds that are secured by pools of mortgages. The investors look to the homeowners' payments, but also to the banks themselves, to guarantee their stream of payments. Around the world, the most common mortgage product is a shorter-term adjustable-rate mortgage.

But David Min noted in congressional testimony that it is "extraordinarily difficult to try to compare different models of housing finance, as these are intrinsically and intricately intertwined with the cultural, political, and economic systems with which they co-exist." For instance, he points out that many Germans rent, instead of own—but the German government offers large rental subsidies. The U.S. is geographically and economically diverse, and for many formative years the country was ideologically opposed to the existence of strong national banks like those that, for instance, fund Canada's mortgage market through deposits. It's impossible to think about our mortgage market without taking these factors into account.

Differences aside, the rest of the world offers no evidence that you can have a mortgage market like that in the U.S., with long-term fixed-rate loans, without some sort of system that guarantees risks investors don't want to take. For consumers, mortgages are commonplace, even mundane. For investors, they are dangerous, very dangerous. Dick Pratt, who was the first president of Merrill Lynch Mortgage Capital, used to say, "The mortgage is the neutron bomb of financial products." Mortgages come packed with risks, including credit risk (the risk that the homeowner won't pay), interest-rate risk (the risk that the lender will earn less on the mortgage than it could get investing its money elsewhere if interest rates rise), and prepayment risk (the risk that a homeowner will pay off a mortgage much earlier than expected, thereby forcing the lender to replace a high-paying asset with a lower-paying one.) Of those risks, the one that most investors like the least is credit risk. The longer the term of the mortgage is, the more risk there is for the lender. And so it's come to be conventional wisdom that a fixture of American life, the 30-year fixed-rate fully prepayable mortgage, would not exist for the wide swath of American consumers but for the presence of companies like Fannie and Freddie, which remove the credit risk and disperse the interest rate and prepayment risk to a wide set of investors. The only other country in the world that offers such a product is tiny Denmark.

It wasn't until the 1960s that Fannie was reborn as what it was originally supposed to be—sort of. It became a private company with all the trappings, including shareholders, stock that could be bought and sold, and a board of directors. This was done because in 1967, during President Lyndon Johnson's administration, a budgetary commission recommended that the debt of agencies like Fannie Mae be included in the federal budget. Adding to the federal debt was no more palatable then than it is today, and so, in 1968, when Johnson signed the Housing and Urban Development Act, he effectively split Fannie in two. The Government National Mortgage Association, or Ginnie Mae, stayed in the government, and guaranteed the credit on only FHA and Veterans Administration mortgages. Fannie Mae, which sold stock to the public, was allowed to guarantee mortgages made to the great American middle class—and its debt stayed off the government's books. "I was in the government when Fannie Mae was a government-owned institution," Paul Volcker later told interviewer Charlie Rose. "And it was created to take care of the mortgage market in times of stress. It was privatized for extraneous reasons. It was privatized to get it out of the budget. Ridiculous."

At the same time, no one wanted to risk hurting Fannie's ability to grease the mortgage market. In his book *The Fateful History of Fannie Mae*, journalist James Hagerty reports that homebuilders raised questions about whether a purely private

68   Fannie would still support the market in hard times. "If you are going to have a private industry, it ought to have certainly a high degree of private control," said Senator John Sparkman, the chairman of the housing subcommittee of the Senate Banking Committee at a hearing in 1968. "But, on the other hand, since this is dealing with matters and programs for which the government has a vested interest, and a vital interest [i.e., homeownership], there ought to be a close connection between the government [and Fannie]. We ought not to divorce it completely."

And so the 1968 legislation gave Fannie some special advantages. One was that federal banks had no limits on the amount they could invest in Fannie's debt, just like government debt. Another was that the U.S. Treasury was authorized to buy up to $2.25 billion of Fannie's debt, thereby sending a signal that this was no ordinary company, but rather one that had the support of the U.S. government. Thus began what Rick Carnell, an assistant Treasury Secretary in the Clinton Administration, described as a "double game." What he meant was that while Fannie and Freddie were ostensibly private companies, their debt was viewed by investors as being akin to U.S. Treasuries, because everyone believed that if necessary, the U.S. government would bail them out.

Securitization: Wall Street Arrives

By 1970, the savings-and-loan industry, which after the Depression had become the primary provider of mortgages—and which was given its most famous portrayal in the 1946 film *It's a Wonderful Life*—had become worried that Fannie was too dominant. The industry pushed for a competitor to which it could sell loans, and that year Congress created the Federal Home Loan Mortgage Corporation, or Freddie Mac. That wasn't enough to save the thrifts, as the old savings-and-loan companies are often called. By the end of the 1970s they were in a state of existential crisis, essentially because they couldn't manage their interest-rate risk in an era of high inflation. In an attempt to fix things, Congress deregulated the thrift industry; the deregulated thrift industry would last less than a decade before it blew up into the savings-and-loan crisis.

Actually, Fannie was in terrible shape too. By the 1980s, it was losing a million dollars a day and "rushing toward a collapse that could have been one of the most disastrous in modern history," as the *Washington Post* later put it. This was also because of interest-rate risk. As interest rates skyrocketed, the mortgages Fannie had bought were paying less than its debt cost. But banks kept lending Fannie money—because they didn't think the government would let it fail. And so it didn't fail.

The market was about to change radically. Wall Street invented a technique called securitization—basically, a way of repackaging mortgages into securities. (There were many fathers of securitization, but the two best known are Lew Ranieri, the Salomon Brothers trader who is considered the godfather of mortgage finance, and Larry Fink, the former First Boston trader who now runs bond giant BlackRock.) In this way, Wall Street firms could step into the GSEs' shoes. Mortgage makers could sell their loans to Street firms, who would then package them up and sell them to investors, with no need for the government.

At least, that's what could have happened, theoretically speaking. But there were laws that made it difficult for investors

70 to buy the new private-label securities, which lacked a Fannie or Freddie stamp. For instance, laws in many states forbade big investors, such as pension funds, from buying securities that lacked that implicit government guarantee.

Wall Street began trying to get the laws changed. And Congress did change some laws. First, in 1986, it passed a law called the Secondary Mortgage Market Enhancement Act. (Ranieri called it the "private sector existence bill," and he warned in congressional testimony that failure to pass it would turn "the mortgage market of America into a totally government franchise.") Among other things, this bill allowed investors to buy securities without a Fannie or Freddie stamp. But even an act of Congress couldn't make investors prefer private-label securities to Fannie or Freddie securities. If they could have a quasi-governmental entity guaranteeing that homeowners would pay, of course that would be better.

The same year, Wall Street tried to get Congress to pass a law that would have given tax advantages to private-label securities. One Reagan Treasury official testified that this law should be "viewed as a first step toward privatization of the secondary mortgage market." But Fannie used its burgeoning political power to stop it in its tracks. In a March 1987 speech to the Mortgage Bankers Association, David Maxwell, who was then Fannie's CEO, said, "They don't seem to care if this would close the door on homeownership for thousands upon thousands of American families." And Fannie called on its friends on Capitol Hill to pressure the Department of Housing and Urban Development to allow it to issue the same securities Wall Street was now selling.

The Roaring Nineties

"Some would say we were too powerful."
—Franklin Raines, CEO of Fannie Mae, 1999–2004

Under the leadership of Jim Johnson, Fannie Mae developed a reputation for playing a kind of political hardball that may have ultimately backfired because of the powerful enemies it made for the company. Johnson, who the *Washington Post* described in a 1998 profile as "one of the most powerful men in the United States," was a born Democratic operative. The son of a member of the Minnesota House of Representatives, he worked on the unsuccessful presidential campaigns of Eugene McCarthy, George McGovern, and Walter Mondale before founding a consulting firm with diplomat Richard Holbrooke. Before joining Fannie in 1990, he was a banker at Lehman Brothers. "I'm not big on losing," he told the *Post*, and it's unclear to this day whether Johnson embraced Fannie's mission of providing homeownership because he believed, or because he understood the political

72   cover it could provide. Maybe it was both. Whatever the reason, he was the primary architect of what former congressman Jim Leach of Iowa once called "the greatest, most sophisticated lobbying operation in the modern history of finance."

The decade of the 1990s at first seemed like a political golden age for Fannie and Freddie. (Freddie, which was much smaller, was mostly happy to follow in Fannie's footsteps.) For years, there were those inside the government, including Leach, who argued that if Fannie and Freddie were to exist at all, they needed better oversight than the Department of Housing and Urban Development could provide. Finally, in 1992, Congress passed a law establishing the Office of Federal Housing Enterprise Oversight, or OFHEO, a regulatory agency whose charge was to oversee just two companies: Fannie and Freddie.

But "OFHEO was structurally weak and almost designed to fail," its director from 1999 to 2005, Armando Falcon, later told the Financial Crisis Inquiry Commission. OFHEO's entire budget, which ranged between $19 million and $30 million during most of the 1990s, was less than the total compensation of the four top executives at Fannie and Freddie, who collectively made $33.6 million in 2000. Treasury official Rick Carnell once described OFHEO as a watchdog that was "hobbled, muzzled, and underfed."

The legislation creating OFHEO did do two critical things. It set capital requirements for the GSEs—but Fannie succeeded in having its capital levels set at a sliver of what bank capital requirements were. It did so by arguing that home mortgages were far less risky than banks' typical business. Tim Howard, a highly intelligent and at times acerbic economist who joined Fannie in

1982 and became its CFO in 1990, helped engage Paul Volcker to conduct an independent analysis in which he agreed that Fannie and Freddie should not have to have as much capital as banks did. In a letter, Volcker wrote, "With [Fannie Mae's] current business practices and assuming it reaches its proposed capital standards, the Company would be in a position to maintain its solvency in the face of difficulties in the housing markets and an interest rate environment significantly more adverse than any experienced in the post-World War II period." Volcker later told journalist James Hagerty that he would probably not have blessed the capital plans "knowing what I know now."

The same legislation established the affordable-housing goals, which required the GSEs to buy, as a percentage of their overall business, certain amounts of loans made to, say, people below the median income level, or people living in rural areas. Fannie executives have always said that the goals were not at all onerous, at least initially. At first, as the General Accounting Office later noted, they were actually *below* HUD's estimates of what the market naturally did already.

During the ensuing years, Fannie and Freddie became extraordinarily profitable and powerful companies. The mortgage market exploded in size, from just under $3 trillion in 1990 to $5.5 trillion by the end of the decade, in part due to the growth in refinancing. Fannie and Freddie, by setting the standards for what kinds of mortgages they would guarantee, effectively determined the sort of mortgage that much of the American middle class would get—and, of course, they took a toll, in the form of a guarantee fee, on every mortgage that passed through them. By the end of the 1990s, Fannie Mae had become America's third-largest corporation, ranked by assets. Freddie was close behind. The companies were ranked one and two respectively on *Fortune*'s list of the most profitable companies per employee. They were deeply woven into the fabric of the financial system. They raised huge quantities of debt to fund their operations, and as a result paid Wall Street big fees. Because their debt was akin to U.S. Treasuries, Fannie and Freddie securities were often used to grease the wheels of Wall Street, for instance as collateral for a derivatives trade. "They were the proverbial 800-pound gorilla," says one mortgage industry veteran. "Wall Street had a love-hate relationship with them. Institutions viewed them as having unfair advantages, and yet they were big clients."

The GSEs were not just forces to be reckoned with domestically, but also internationally. In 1985, Fannie had begun borrowing money from abroad to finance its purchases of mortgages. Foreign central banks soon became big buyers of Fannie- and Freddie-backed mortgage securities, too. In the mid-1990s, as the days when the U.S. ran a budget deficit appeared to be coming to an end, Fannie decided to begin offering what it called Benchmark Notes. In effect, these were an attempt to substitute its debt for the debt of the United States: After all, if there wasn't going to be any more U.S. debt, couldn't Fannie take advantage of investors' desire for a super-safe investment by selling them its own debt instead? In 1999, Fannie sold $114 billion in Benchmark securities, with more than one-third going to foreign investors. The Financial Crisis Inquiry Commission later reported that in 1998, foreign holdings of Fannie and Freddie securities were about what they had been in the previous decade—$186 billion. By 2000—just two years later—foreigners owned $348 billion in Fannie and Freddie securities; by 2004, they owned $875 billion. At the time, it seemed brilliant to have foreign money financing the most domestic asset—homes—there is. The downside would only become apparent in crisis time, when policy makers realized that the presence of foreign investors was one reason they had to do what they always said they wouldn't, which was stand behind the GSEs.

For all the problems—the lack of capital, the arrogance, the political maneuvering—that would later seem so obvious, Fannie and Freddie, with the help of the U.S. government, accomplished something that Rumpelstiltskin would envy. They took the worst possible investment—a 30-year fixed-rate fully prepayable mortgage—and turned it into the second most liq uid instrument in the world, just behind Treasuries. (Liquidity, which means that investors know they can easily buy and sell something, is highly valued in the financial world.) They equalized the flow of credit, so that a wide variety of factors in this country, from geography to income levels, didn't affect a consumer's ability to get a mortgage or even the rate they would pay. Fannie Mae and Freddie Mac were long viewed by many as shining examples of public-private partnership—that is, the harnessing of private capital to advance a social good: in this case, homeownership.

It didn't look like there was any end in sight. "In Johnson's last years, everyone wanted to be there, everyone wanted to share our aura, everyone wanted our money, everyone wanted to be part of Fannie Mae," says Bill Maloni, who was a Fannie Mae lobbyist for more than 20 years. "We were on Everest up until 2003." And then, he says, "We went to Death Valley."

"We Were at War"

"If you were looking for the absolutely best way to mine money out of the government, it was brilliantly designed to do just that. I'm not sure they figured it out, or if they just took advantage of opportunities."
—Larry Summers, Director of the National Economic Council, 2009–2010

In late 1998, Jim Johnson stepped down. His handpicked successor was Franklin Delano Raines, who had grown up in Seattle, where his father was a custodian for the city parks department, and his mother was a cleaning woman for Boeing—a company on whose board Raines would later serve. Raines was a star. He earned a scholarship to Harvard, was named a Rhodes Scholar, interned in the Nixon White House, and then served in the Carter Administration before leaving to become a partner at Lazard Frères, where he spent the next eleven years. After his first stint at Fannie Mae, from 1991 to 1996, he became the head of the Office of Management and Budget at the beginning of Bill Clinton's second term. Raines reaped enormous credit for balancing the budget. When he returned to Fannie Mae in 1998—with a promise from Johnson that he could soon take it over—his political stock could not have been higher. There was talk that he would be the first black president of the United States.

Raines, while at Harvard, was a member of both the Young Democrats and the Young Republicans. He'd later joke that Vice President Al Gore suspected he was a Republican because of his focus on the budget. But like Johnson, he was indeed a Democrat, as were many top Fannie executives, and the fact that Democratic operatives made fortunes at Fannie fed into a subterranean resentment of both companies—a resentment that would soon burst to the surface.

Many economists, including liberal economists, have never been entirely comfortable with the concept of a government-backed private company. Larry Summers, the economist who served as Treasury Secretary in the Clinton Administration and became the head of the National Economic Council in the Obama Administration, said: "If you were looking for a way to extract rents from the government, what would you do? Well, first, you would have it be as non-transparent as possible. So you'd have an implicit guarantee. You would do your best to staple the rents to a broad middle class subsidy so you couldn't attack the rents without also attacking the middle class subsidy. The third thing is, you would make yourself a source of positive opportunity for opportunistic politicians."

Even in the Johnson years, there were little rebellions against the GSEs' growing power, which were mostly squelched. In 1996, Ed DeMarco, then an economist at the Treasury, was the chief author of a report that was more critical of Fannie and Freddie than most people dared to be. (DeMarco, who had previously been at the Government Accountability Office, had also written a report recommending much stronger regulation for the GSEs.) The last chapter recommended various ways in which Fannie and Freddie could be severed from the government. But the final version of the report lacked that chapter, as well as other critical parts. In Tim Howard's book, he writes that it was Summers who edited the tough report. But a former Treasury official says the report was changed because the analysis didn't pass the review process, not because of the conclusions. Certainly, Summers would prove to be no friend of Fannie and Freddie.

Several things brought the resentment to a fever pitch. By the late 1990s, the substantial profits that Fannie and Freddie were reporting were not just from their traditional business of stamping mortgages with a guarantee and collecting a fee in exchange. Increasingly, both Fannie and Freddie had begun to buy up their own mortgage-backed securities and hold them on their balance sheet. Because of their special position, they could make money on the difference between higher yield of the mortgage portfolio and what their cost of funds was. The "big fat gap" is what Alan Greenspan, the very powerful chairman of the Federal Reserve for almost two decades, until 2006, took to calling it. The GSEs' combined portfolios would peak in 2008 at a stunning $1.6 trillion. To put that in context, at the end of 2007, the entire public federal debt stood at around $9 trillion.

As the portfolios grew, they provided critics with a convenient target. After all, what did they do besides mint money for the GSEs' shareholders and executives? And due to all the interest-rate risk that Fannie and Freddie were holding on their balance sheet—and all the derivatives they were using to manage that interest-rate risk—weren't they a disaster waiting to happen, a disaster that would land on taxpayers? Among critics of Fannie and Freddie, an oft-repeated line was that they privatized gains—those went to shareholders and executives—while socializing losses.

Surprisingly, given the prominent Democrats at Fannie, it was the Clinton Treasury that first took on Fannie and Freddie in an organized way, when Gary Gensler, an assistant Treasury Secretary who would later become the chairman of the Commodities Futures Trading Commission, said, among other things, that the U.S. Treasury should cut the GSEs' $2.5 billion line of credit. Yields on Fannie and Freddie debt soared, meaning that investors now saw the debt as much riskier. Tim Howard called Gensler's comments "inappropriate" and "unprofessional." Fannie took to describing itself as a "bulwark of our financial system."

Gene Sperling, who was the director of the National Economic Council, says that he, Summers, and Gensler had agreed to stand strong together. "I thought it was a moment of pride in doing the right thing, not the politically convenient thing," he says today. They began making other comments that suggested a lack of true government support for Fannie and Freddie. Sperling, who considers himself a progressive, marvels today: "The GSEs brought out a conservative side of me. The thing that turned me, that made me unwilling to do anything personally for them, is when you see that dynamic where a company is completely dependent on the U.S. government for their profit and they spend so much money and time focused on lobbying the U.S. government. It really gets kind of sick." He used to joke: "If you think a bad thought about Fannie and Freddie, you can hear the fax machine going."

Greenspan, for a while, was quieter. But inside Fannie, it wasn't any secret that the powerful Fed chairman was opposed to them too. "I knew the Fed thought of Fannie as a tar baby," says Raines. "When I came back to Fannie, it was clear that we were at war." Greenspan still came to Raines's annual Christmas parties, and Raines says he made a point of going to see Greenspan, bringing with him presentations that explained how Fannie managed its risk. (Greenspan would later call the explanations "nonsense.") But, says Raines, "Greenspan is a great maneuverer and he was maneuvering to get the Fed positioned to take on Fannie."

The stew of distaste and envy was compounded by questions about what value Fannie and Freddie actually provided. The Congressional Budget Office produced study after study showing that the subsidy wasn't going to homebuyers; instead, it was going to shareholders and executives. After one study estimated that about 40 percent of Fannie and Freddie's profits were due to their implied government support, a Fannie spokesman denounced the report, calling it the work of "economic pencil brains who wouldn't recognize something that works for ordinary homebuyers if it bit them in their erasers." Raines would often argue that the private-market cost for a mortgage was 25 to 50 basis points more than the Fannie Mae price, or a quarter to half a percent. What the GSEs never advertised was an "average" figure was somewhat misleading. Because for years, everyone who qualified for a Fannie or Freddie mortgage paid a similar rate; what the GSEs really were was a giant subsidization machine, where wealthier borrowers in desirable areas paid more than they otherwise would have, while less well-off borrowers in less desirable locations paid less than they otherwise would have.

Oddly enough, the steps the GSEs took to fulfill their affordable-housing mandates were a cause of controversy too—although for exactly the opposite reason that they became controversial after the crisis. In 1994, Jim Johnson announced, with great fanfare, that by the end of the decade Fannie would make $1 trillion available to finance housing for "minorities, low and moderate income families, new immigrants, families who live in central cities and distressed areas, and people with special housing needs." By the mid-1990s Fannie and Freddie were guaranteeing loans with down payments as low as 3 percent, which is shocking to anyone who grew up in the era where you needed a 20 percent down payment. But these were not the sort of crazy loans that would become so prevalent by the mid-2000s. They were long-term fixed-rate mortgages made to people who fully documented their income, and Fannie often insisted that borrowers undergo financial counseling. The default rate on these loans was, as you'd expect, higher than on prime loans, but the overall default rate remained very low.

At the time, the controversy was that despite all these programs, Fannie and Freddie didn't do enough for the cause of affordable housing. One critic was John Taylor, the president of the access-to-credit advocacy association National Community Reinvestment Coalition. Another was the conservative economist Peter Wallison, who now blames Fannie and Freddie's pursuit of the affordable-housing goals for the financial crisis. In an introduction to a 2004 book that recommended privatizing Fannie and Freddie, Wallison wrote that their "extensive advertising has created the false impression that they are essential to the provision of affordable housing to disadvantaged groups. As many studies have shown, however, they lag ordinary banks in this respect." He continued: "Study after study has shown that Fannie Mae and Freddie Mac, despite full-throated claims about trillion-dollar commitments and the like, have failed to lead the private market in assisting the development and financing of affordable housing." (Wallison now says that he, like others, just wasn't aware that Fannie and Freddie actually were leading the market.)

Fannie played hardball even here. Taylor recalls getting a commitment from Fannie for a small grant. After he testified at a congressional hearing that the company didn't do enough for affordable housing, he got a call from a Fannie executive who told him that they had run out of money. Taylor says he picked up the phone and called Jim Johnson. "I said, 'You have to tell me that Fannie is not that small minded,'" he says. The grant was reestablished. Wallison, who served on the board of a mortgage insurer until 1999, later alleged that pressure from Fannie led to his resignation from the board.

In 1999, Raines announced that Fannie would begin buying some subprime mortgages—generally more expensive mortgages made to people with less than pristine credit. Fannie executives still argue that they were helping borrowers who were very close to qualifying for a Fannie Mae loan, but would otherwise have been shoved into a more expensive subprime product. "This was a follow-the-market innovation," says another executive, who notes that at the time, Fannie released a strict set of standards that barred it from purchasing many of the subprime loans the private sector was making. "I would get yelled at because I was saying, 'We'll take the top end,'" Raines says today. "Because people didn't belong there. But we were told to stay out."

Indeed, others in the mortgage industry worried that Fannie and Freddie were controlling more and more of the market. Around the same time, a group of private mortgage companies launched an organization called FM Watch, which dedicated itself to reining in Fannie and Freddie. Its initial sponsors were three large bank-owned mortgage lenders (Chase Mortgage, Wells Fargo, and PNC Mortgage), one subprime lender (Household Financial), and GE and AIG, the parent companies of two mortgage insurers. FM Watch also argued that Fannie didn't "want to risk its profit margins by doing as much as it should to serve affordable housing." Fannie, in turn, labeled FM Watch "The Coalition for Higher Mortgage Costs."

The $9 Billion Accounting Fraud

"American consumers might benefit if lenders provided greater mortgage product alternatives to the traditional fixed-rate mortgages."
—Alan Greenspan, Chairman of the Federal Reserve, 1987–2006

Early in his second term as president, Bill Clinton announced his National Homeownership Strategy. It had an explicit goal of raising the number of homeowners by 8 million families over the next six years. To get there, the administration advocated "financing strategies fueled by creativity to help home buyers who lacked the cash to buy a home or the income to make the down payments."

When George W. Bush became president in 2000, he showed no sign of stepping back from Clinton's strategy. Quite the opposite: during Bush's campaign, part of the Republican Party platform was that "homeownership is central to the American Dream."

But Hank Paulson, the Goldman Sachs executive who would
serve as Bush's third Treasury Secretary, later wrote this about
the president: "He had a deep disdain for entities like Fannie
and Freddie, which he saw as a part of a permanent Washington
elite, detached from the heartland, with former government
officials and lobbyists cycling through their ranks endlessly
while the companies minted money, thanks, in effect, to a federal entitlement." And there were others in the White House, including some on the National Economic Council, who were long
time GSE critics and were just hoping for a way to rein them in.

The spark that lit the fire was the Enron scandal, which
put its accountant, Arthur Andersen, out of business. After
that, Freddie Mac, which had also employed Andersen, hired
PricewaterhouseCoopers. The new accountants scrubbed
Freddie's books—and in 2003, Freddie admitted that it had un-
derstated its profits for years in an effort to produce the smooth
earnings that investors like to see. The company agreed to a $5
billion restatement and ousted many of its top executives.

It was a huge embarrassment for the beleaguered OFHEO,
which had signed off on Freddie's safety and soundness just
months before the announcement. OFHEO's director by then
was Armando Falcon, a Texas Democrat. Instead of accepting
Fannie's assurances that its accounts were just fine, in early
2004, Falcon hired the accounting firm Deloitte to do an investigation of Fannie.

All at once, what had been sporadic, fairly uncoordinated
efforts to rein in the GSEs became a concerted push with the
force of the government behind it. The Bush Administration
made common cause with Falcon and began ramping up a push

86   for new, stronger regulation of Fannie and Freddie. Later, Raines and his lawyers even subpoenaed the White House to try to find what his lawyers called "evidence that officials in the most powerful office in the country were part of a plan to influence the political debate about Fannie Mae."

Greenspan, with support from the administration, began to testify in Congress about the risks the GSEs, particularly their huge portfolios of mortgages, posed to the financial system. He wasn't worried about credit risk—the risk that homeowners wouldn't pay their mortgages. At the time, no one thought that was a risk. Instead, he was worried about all the derivatives Fannie and Freddie used to manage the interest-rate risk on those huge portfolios. His sharpest comments came in early 2004, when he told Congress that "to fend off possible future systemic difficulties, which we assess as likely if G.S.E. expansion continues unabated, preventative actions are required sooner rather than later, according to Tim Howard."

Greenspan also seemingly went out of his way to question the wisdom of consumers' preference for financing their homes with 30-year fixed-rate mortgages—the loan type that comprised over 90 percent of Fannie Mae's business at the time. He said, "American consumers might benefit if lenders provided greater mortgage product alternatives to the traditional fixed-rate mortgages."

For years, Congressman Richard Baker of Louisiana had been one of the few lonely voices questioning Fannie and Freddie, but he was now joined by Republican Senator Richard Shelby of Alabama. Mark Calabria, who was then a staffer for Shelby, later explained in a paper that Shelby told his staff he wanted a GSE regulator that was as "bank-like" as possible, with the ability to impose strong capital conditions and to place a failing GSE into either conservatorship, in an effort to conserve their assets and restore them to a safe and sound financial condition, or receivership, which was a procedure for reorganizing Fannie or Freddie in the event of a bankruptcy.

Calabria later wrote that as they tried to hammer out a bill, of particular importance were the large holdings of Fannie and Freddie debt by foreign governments, especially foreign banks. He wrote: "Some of these central banks, such as the Chinese and Russian, have unique and critical relationships with the United States. These central banks are also large purchasers of U.S. Treasury debt. The Banking Committee was not unaware of these relationships. In fact concerns were repeatedly voiced that if left to the Treasury, credit losses on GSE debt holders by foreign central banks would be transferred to the American taxpayer. This was viewed as an unacceptable outcome."

By setting up a receivership mechanism, the government would be sending an unmistakable message: It would not stand behind Fannie and Freddie's debt. That, of course, would negate Fannie's most powerful advantage, which was its low cost of funds.

Initially, Fannie's political power frustrated even the White House's attempts to rein in the GSEs. "It was the height of how influential we were," a former GSE lobbyist recalls. "Raines said, 'We can't support something that changes the deal for bondholders.' So Fannie convinced Bennett [Republican Senator Bob Bennett of Utah] and Enzi [Republican Senator Mike Enzi of Wyoming] to sponsor an amendment." The amendment gave

88   Congress a 45-day window to veto the receivership. That completely undercut the notion that the government would no longer back the GSEs.

The former lobbyist recalls that Fannie executives showed a roomful of Democrats a report from Standard & Poor's, which said the agency might cut its rating on Fannie's debt should the bill pass, because the debt would no longer be regarded as super-safe. Raines explained to the assembled Democrats that that would hurt the commercial banks in their areas, because they all held Fannie and Freddie debt, and they would have to take losses if the rating were cut. The Democrats all supported Bennett and Enzi's amendment, and as a result Shelby pulled his badly weakened bill.

In April 2004, the *Wall Street Journal* published a story that discussed many ways that the administration could weaken the GSEs. "Frustrated by its inability to win congressional approval to tighten regulation of mortgage giants Fannie Mae and Freddie Mac, the government is pursuing the same goal through regulatory fiat," it said.

One of the things the Bush Administration did was to have HUD ramp up the GSEs' affordable-housing goals—the amount of business Fannie and Freddie were required to do with low- and moderate-income borrowers—to significantly higher levels to make sure that they were actually delivering on the obligations in their charters, and to make sure that Fannie and Freddie understood who was boss in the relationship.

But it was OFHEO that would do in Fannie. On September 22, 2004, OFHEO released the results of its accounting examination. Part of the report alleged that Fannie's management had improperly shifted expenses from one year to the next in order to meet bonus targets for its executives, but the majority of the report was focused on Fannie's misuse of a complicated new accounting statute governing how gains and losses from derivatives are recorded. It was too dense for most people to follow the details, but the outcome was clear: OFHEO said that Fannie had overstated its earnings by $9 billion since 2001, representing a staggering 40 percent of its profits. In a letter to the Fannie Mae board accompanying the report, Armando Falcon wrote: "These findings cannot be explained as mere differences in interpretation of accounting principles, but clear instances in which management sought to misapply and ignore accounting principles for the purposes of meeting investment analyst expectations [and] reducing volatility in reported earnings." Management, of course, was Franklin Raines and Tim Howard.

Fannie tried to fight back—after all, its accountants, PricewaterhouseCoopers, had signed off on its financial statements. Raines was so confident that the company had done nothing wrong that he took the unique step of going to the Securities and Exchange Commission for an independent judgment. But the final blow came when the Securities and Exchange Commission's chief accountant, Donald Nicolaisen, weighed in. In a meeting at the SEC's offices, he held up a sheet of paper. If the four corners represented what was possible under accounting rules and the center was perfect compliance, he told Raines, "You weren't even on the page."

By the end of the year, both Raines and Howard were gone from Fannie. OFHEO later filed charges against both men, and also against another Fannie executive, seeking more than $215 million in bonus payments and fines. Fannie was ordered by OFHEO to restate its earnings from 2001 through 2004. Falcon even called Fannie Mae a "government-sponsored Enron." Both the SEC and the Department of Justice launched investigations.

A $9 billion accounting fraud is a major story, and for months Fannie Mae was all over the headlines. And the number was soon revised upward, to almost $11 billion.

Fannie didn't go down without a fight. Bill Maloni, the Fannie lobbyist, got Kit Bond, a Republican senator from Missouri, to launch an investigation into OFHEO. The resulting report was highly unusual, at least if you expect a regulator to care about the welfare of the companies it regulates. The report said that OFHEO had a "very strong intent to embarrass Fannie Mae." Falcon's special counsel, a man named Steve Blumenthal, responded to one e-mail chain with an apparent non sequitur. "Fannie and Freddie are the axis of evil and must be destroyed," he wrote. "Get with the program." Both OFHEO's chief accountant, Wanda DeLeo, and its chief examiner, Scott Calhoun, complained that Falcon and his special counsel were overstating Fannie's problems for political impact.

Fannie always argued that the accounting issue wasn't caused by malfeasance, and that there was no hidden loss. When Fannie finally released its restated numbers at the end of 2006, shareholders' equity, which is the most important measure of a company's health, had actually increased by $4.1 billion over the contested period from 2002 until mid-2004. David Fiderer, who was an early skeptic about OFHEO's case, later wrote that "after the overblown media narrative about Fannie Mae's accounting problems had calcified into the zeitgeist, almost no one looked

at the numbers and asked where they came from. By every standard metric—cumulative net income, shareholder's equity, cor-
porate cash flows—Fannie's financial position turned out to be
far stronger than originally reported."

Both Raines and Howard settled OFHEO's charges, but neither man admitted guilt. Most of their combined $31 million
settlement consisted of worthless stock options that OFHEO
valued at their grant prices, rather than at the actual stock price
at the time, in order to arrive at a grand-sounding number. "In an
ironic way, it was a fitting climax: a suit that began with OFHEO
accusing us of deliberate fraud ended with OFHEO putting a deliberately fraudulent value on what we paid to settle it," Howard
wrote in his book. Both the SEC and the Justice Department
quietly dropped their investigations.

And finally, in the fall of 2012, after eight years, 67 million
pages of documents, and testimony from over 150 witnesses, a
civil suit against Howard, Raines, and another executive ended
with the federal judge dismissing all the charges. He concluded
that there was no evidence that either Raines or Howard had
purposefully tried to deceive anyone. The SEC's former chief
accountant, Nicolaisen, was deposed. Fiderer reported that he
seemed to be more equivocal than he had been back in 2004. As
it turned out, many other companies had done their accounting
the way Fannie did. "What I expressed was my view and professional judgment," Nicolaisen said. "In my opinion, it was outside the professional bounds. But that is an opinion. I mean,
I'll be very clear also in saying a lot of other people concluded
otherwise." Today, Nicolaisen says that in the wake of a string
of accounting scandals in the early 2000s, including Enron, he

92   was "very frustrated" with the accounting-and-audit profession and was trying to draw a strong line about what was acceptable and what wasn't. But, he says, he was opining only on how Fannie had implemented a complex accounting rule and not whether anyone at Fannie had purposefully done anything wrong. About Raines, he says, "My impression was that he intended that Fannie comply fully with the relevant accounting standards."

The result of all this was a complete tangle: Fannie and Freddie's stable management was gone; their institutional reputations were badly tarnished; but no one among the GSEs' many critics had the nerve—or the political support—to create anything positive out of the mess. Although Senator Shelby tried again to pass new, much tougher legislation governing Fannie and Freddie, he couldn't do it, even with a Republican White House and Congress. So the GSEs rolled on, deeply wounded, with thin levels of capital and ever more onerous requirements to put their stamp on riskier loans as the mortgage market entered its most dangerous period in history, until it all crashed and government conservatorship began.

Limbo

Part Three

The Toxic Twins

"It was amazing how little actual authority we had over Fannie
and Freddie considering they were entirely dependent on
Treasury's cash to stay alive."
—Timothy Geithner, Secretary of the Treasury, 2009–2013

Just after Fannie and Freddie were put into conservatorship, Jim
Lockhart stepped down as the director of the new agency created to regulate them. He left as acting director Ed DeMarco,
the free-market economist who had worked with him on
privatizing Social Security—and who had previously recommended the privatization of Fannie and Freddie. While the
Obama Administration did try to replace DeMarco, the politics
around any appointment that required congressional approval
quickly became a manifestation of the increasingly poisonous
atmosphere in Washington. And so DeMarco would end up
staying in his job for almost six years.

The situation was strange, even by the standards of the GSEs. As a Fannie employee says drily, "It is unusual for a regulator to have a strong point of view that is antithetical to the existence of your regulatee." That wasn't the only oddity. DeMarco was a longtime civil servant, and on the surface he appeared to be exactly what you'd expect: mild-mannered and academic. But now he was effectively the CEO of a $5 trillion enterprise on a government salary. Most unusual of all is that DeMarco had a crystal-clear view of what his job as conservator was, and that was to protect taxpayers. There's an argument that that was not precisely what the law governing conservatorship said (the mandate was to "conserve and preserve" the companies' assets), but DeMarco would hold true to his view in the face of extraordinary pressure.

In the beginning, it was triage. The market was crashing, home prices were plummeting, and almost everyone thought Fannie and Freddie would be an endless black hole. Quarter after quarter, they posted stunning multibillion dollar losses, which required huge draws from Treasury. In early 2009, the Treasury amended its agreement to increase the total amount of funding available for Fannie and Freddie from $200 billion to $400 billion—half the 10-year estimated cost of Obamacare. On Christmas Eve, 2009, the Treasury amended the agreement again to remove any cap on the funding for the next three years. In addition, the Federal Reserve began to buy Fannie and Freddie securities to help the perception that they were safe. According to Paul Willen, a senior economist at the Boston Federal Reserve, between 2008 and 2014 the Fed would purchase $2.8 trillion of agency mortgage-backed securities.

Employees of Fannie and Freddie, now dubbed the "Toxic Twins," were demoralized by the flood of criticism, and under the terms of the conservatorship they weren't allowed to say anything to defend themselves. They weren't allowed to lobby, or even go to conferences, talk to academics or thought leaders, write op-eds, or attend outside meetings without permission (which, says an employee, was often withheld). "We had no voice," says a former executive. "So the philosophy was, 'Head down, focus on what you can do. We do not want the company to be remembered this way. We've got to fix this.'"

Private capital totally disappeared from the mortgage market. By the end of the year, Fannie and Freddie, along with Ginnie Mae, accounted for about 97 percent of mortgage-backed securities issuance, according to the Government Accountability Office.

Over the next few years, Treasury and Fannie and Freddie would roll out a variety of programs to try various ways to help people stay in their homes. In the beginning especially, the programs didn't work very well. This led to fury because, in people's minds, the government, which had done so much to help the banks, wasn't doing enough to help homeowners.

There were bitter battles over these programs. The biggest one was over principal reduction, or whether the administration should enable the write-down of mortgages that were larger than the value of the homes. By the fourth quarter of 2009, according to research firm CoreLogic, 24 percent of borrowers, or 11.3 million mortgages, owed more than their homes were worth, for a total of around $700 billion in negative equity. The numbers would get worse before they got better. Many

borrowers will walk away from their mortgage in such circum-
stances; the default hurts the borrower, the lender, and everyone else in the neighborhood when the now-empty house gets
trashed. So why not have a program that forgave the amount of
the loan that was greater than the value of the house?

The fight over principal forgiveness became one of the ug-
liest parts of the post-crisis landscape. Republicans were opposed to it. The prospect that the government would bail out
borrowers became a spark for the Tea Party movement. There
were a lot of real issues, despite the headline appeal of principal forgiveness. Take two neighbors, one of whom borrowed
responsibly, and one of whom did a cash-out refinancing in order to buy a boat and go on vacation. How does the first feel if
he gets nothing, while the second has his debt forgiven? Next,
who was going to pay for it? Investors? Taxpayers? There was
$50 billion in the Troubled Asset Relief Program that was sup-
posed to be dedicated to keeping people in their homes. Most of
it hadn't been spent, which was a source of great anger among
progressives. But even $50 billion wouldn't buy much.

Initially, it seemed that the administration and DeMarco
were of the same skeptical view. Obama's political team was
afraid that principal reduction would feed into the narrative that
the president wasn't out to protect the responsible middle class
but just the rich and the poor, according to a former official. Yet
by 2011, a lot had changed. The entire progressive base fixated
on principal reduction as *the* issue. The lack of it began to feed
a narrative of unfairness to the little guy, in contrast to the lar-
gesse given to the big banks. That there was money at all left in
TARP was a constant source of criticism of the administration.

98   Why hadn't it been used to help struggling homeowners? The political team began to believe it was important to fire up the base before the election, says a former official. Most of all, President Obama very much wanted action. Treasury Secretary Timothy Geithner had originally been opposed to principal reduction, but his team began to argue that it could make sense for a targeted set of underwater borrowers with Fannie- and Freddie-backed loans, and Geithner came around to that view.

DeMarco did not agree. In 2012, he got a call from Treasury, which told him that it was going to use the leftover TARP money to triple the incentives offered to investors to do principal reductions. So he should get with the program too. DeMarco said he'd study it, and study it he did. Fannie and Freddie's analysis showed that under a best-case scenario, principal reduction could save money, because borrowers would pay their reduced mortgages instead of defaulting. But as soon as you factored in even a small number of people who were paying their mortgages but would choose not to as soon as they had the option—this is called strategic default—the program quickly imposed a significant loss on taxpayers. Almost 90 percent of homeowners with a GSE-guaranteed mortgage were paying. (Indeed, according to a Congressional Budget Office analysis, while Fannie and Freddie owned or guaranteed some 60 percent of outstanding mortgages, they had only 30 percent of the underwater mortgages.) Why risk a hit to taxpayers?

So on July 31, 2012, DeMarco said he wouldn't do principal reduction. He'd shared all of FHFA's analysis with Treasury. Less than ten minutes later, Geithner fired back a letter saying that the GSEs' own analysis showed that principal reduction

could help up to half a million borrowers and save several billion dollars. The core difference was in their views of the risk
of strategic defaults, which Treasury argued was minimal. "You
have the power to help more struggling homeowners and heal
the remaining damage from the housing crisis," Geithner wrote
to DeMarco. But DeMarco would not budge.

Treasury officials, and at least some of the National
Economic Council economists, thought DeMarco's view was
ridiculously narrow. Taxpayers, after all, would benefit from
what benefited the broader economy. "The White House
couldn't believe it," says a former official. "You've got the NEC,
HUD, and Treasury saying, 'These are the numbers,' and this
guy who is not even confirmed is completely blocking us. There
was nothing we could do." Geithner was furious. By the fall of
2012, people were picketing outside DeMarco's modest house
in Silver Spring, Maryland, chanting "Ed DeMarco, we're coming for you." *Time* ran a story headlined, "Is This Man Single-
Handedly Stifling the U.S. Housing Recovery?" In 2013, a group
of state attorneys general publicly called on President Obama to
fire DeMarco.

The widespread view of Ed DeMarco was that he was just a
right-wing lapdog who was morally opposed to principal reduction. But that's as much a misreading of him as it would be to
argue that he was trying to help save Fannie and Freddie by lim-
iting their losses. What he was trying to do was to save taxpayers
money. He might well have been right. Economist Paul Willen
argues that for struggling borrowers, it is much more important
to reduce monthly payments than it is to reduce principal, and
Fannie and Freddie have done that.

(You can see proof of DeMarco's determination to mini-
mize the losses to taxpayers in something else he did. In 2011,
DeMarco's FHFA sued 18 big banks, seeking to recover losses
on a total of roughly $200 billion in private-label securities that
the banks had sold to Fannie and Freddie. The lawsuits alleged
that the banks had violated securities laws and, in some in-
stances, committed fraud, because the quality of the underlying
mortgages in their securities was so much worse than they had
represented. Although most banks settled—to date, Fannie and
Freddie have collected roughly $18 billion in settlements—they
complained bitterly that the FHFA was being far too aggressive
and insisted that they did nothing wrong, a stance that mirrors
their overall defense of their behavior during the boom. Two
banks, Nomura Securities and the Royal Bank of Scotland, even
took the case to trial, providing a rare public airing of their behavior. In a scathing 361-page decision, Judge Denise Cote of the
Federal District Court in Manhattan ruled against them. "The
magnitude of falsity, conservatively measured, is enormous,"
she wrote.)

Still, as time went on, you could see that DeMarco, true
as he was to his responsibilities as he defined them, certainly
hadn't changed his underlying views on Fannie and Freddie. "Ed
started as a good little civil servant and at first it was, 'I'll just
try to keep the lights on and you tell me what to do,'" says someone who knows him well. "But bit by bit, he got more aggressive, because he got frustrated by the lack of a broader policy." A
former Fannie executive explains DeMarco this way: "At some
point, Ed said, 'You're not going to be able to get rid of me. I'm
the conservator. If no one is making policy, I'll make policy!'"

Everything DeMarco did seemed to be designed to prepare the mortgage markets for the day when Fannie and Freddie no longer existed. (Which was in keeping with what the administration was saying it wanted.) For example, Fannie and Freddie began to build a new system for turning mortgages into securities, one that would be available to anyone, so that when private investors came back to the mortgage market, they could simply plug into it. Under DeMarco's prodding, the GSEs steadily increased their guarantee fees for new mortgages. Fannie Mae's average effective guarantee fee on new loans tripled from 21 basis points in the first quarter of 2009 to 63 basis points in the first quarter of 2014. In December 2013, DeMarco proposed another hike in guarantee fees. He also began charging extra fees for riskier mortgages in order to decrease the amount of cross-subsidization in the system. The whole idea was that as the cost of Fannie and Freddie's insurance policy rose, the private sector would see an opportunity to make money, and come back into the market.

"DeMarco is very smart," says Franklin Raines. "He pushed the ball further and did more to reduce Fannie's and Freddie's role in the future than anyone else." He adds: "It was brilliant. I thought he'd get away with it."

Doing Nothing

"I hope by next year we'll have abolished Fannie and Freddie."
—Barney Frank, Chairman of the House Financial Services
Committee, 2007–2011, on *The Larry Kudlow Show*, August 2010

By 2010, everyone, even those who had been longtime Fannie
and Freddie supporters, from President Obama to Paul Volcker,
agreed with what Senator Barney Frank, then the chairman of
the House Financial Services Committee, said on *The Larry
Kudlow Show* in August of that year. The rhetoric certainly made
it sound like the U.S. government had finally decided to kill
its Frankensteins.

But while there was no shortage of suggestions about how
to do away with Fannie and Freddie, it would not prove easy to
implement any of them. "Making policy on this was one of the
hardest things by an order of magnitude for the administration,"
says a former official. "The danger is that it leads to all kinds of

narratives that feel good but ultimately don't lend themselves to reality. It's fucking terrible to explain to the public. Both the politics and substance are much more complicated than anyone expected." He adds: "And if you get the substance wrong, it could be really problematic. This is a major segment of the economy supporting the major asset most Americans have."

Even steps that might seem obvious are replete with hidden problems. For instance, if you were to abolish Fannie and Freddie, what would happen to the existing $5 trillion in GSE-backed securities? There would be a tidal wave of selling as investors realized that those existing securities no longer had government backing. Foreign investors would be furious. You could swap Fannie and Freddie securities for Treasuries, but then you'd have to put it all on the government balance sheet, which would make the federal government's debt look much bigger. If you started hiking guarantee fees, people with good credit would get a cheaper mortgage elsewhere, thereby leaving the weaker credits to Fannie and Freddie. Also, we were in the middle of a housing crisis. Why would you want to exacerbate the problem? Housing accounts for nearly 20 percent of the American economy. Despite the decline in home prices since the crisis, primary residences still accounted for almost 30 percent of family assets in 2010, according to the Federal Reserve. In a quaking economy, who wants to risk curtailing, or even reducing, the flow of credit enabled by Fannie and Freddie? "It's a perennial problem," says a former Obama Administration economist. "You can't do anything to make the housing market worse at the moment when it just imploded. Even the GSEs' biggest critics weren't saying, 'Do this next year.'"

It would soon become clear that as much as people theoretically wanted to get rid of Fannie and Freddie, very few were
actually willing to pull the plug, particularly if they would have
to take responsibility for whatever happened next. Another
economist who worked in the administration recalls being in a
meeting where senior people were discussing a status change to
Fannie and Freddie. Someone said, "No, you can't do that, you'll
freak out foreign investors, you'll rock the market." This person
recalls thinking, "Then we can't do anything. Ever."

A small episode in early 2010 demonstrated the conun-
drum. Barney Frank pointed out that Fannie and Freddie had
something less than full government backing. (Which was,
and is, true. A line of credit is not the same thing as full backing.) He said: "People who own Fannie and Freddie debt are not
in the same legal position as [those who own] Treasury bonds,
and I don't want them to be." Concerned that Frank's comments
would spook foreign investors, the Treasury promptly issued a
statement. "There should be no uncertainty about Treasury's
commitment to support Fannie Mae and Freddie Mac as they
continue to play a vital role in the housing market during this
current crisis," it read.

For these reasons, it was always pretty clear that Democrats
wouldn't include Fannie and Freddie in the Dodd-Frank Wall
Street Reform and Consumer Protection Act. One item about
Fannie and Freddie did make it into the bill, which required
Treasury to study and submit recommendations to Congress on
Fannie and Freddie reform.

Geithner, according to several former officials, wasn't
an ideologue. In fact, he, along with Gene Sperling, who in

early 2011 replaced Larry Summers as the head of the National Economic Council, believed that there was simply no practical way to get the government out of the mortgage market. That spring, in a congressional hearing, Geithner broadly endorsed some kind of government role in the housing market, although he was unclear on how expansive it should be. Part of his argument was that in the event of another financial crisis, it was important to have a toolkit in place that could mitigate the downturn, and one critical part of that was the ability to expand Fannie and Freddie's market share. It wouldn't be feasible to ramp up the government's role from zero.

There were several other arguments within the administration for a broader government presence. One was that because of the centrality of housing, if and when the housing market imploded, the government would be on the hook anyway; so in the meantime, the government might as well collect fees for explicitly insuring some sort of backstop. Another was that without an implicit or explicit government guarantee, the price for a 30-year mortgage for the wide swath of the American middle class would be far higher, if it were available at all.

But there was no consensus. Before the Treasury study was due, there was a meeting with President Obama that was quite fittingly held in the Roosevelt Room, with a giant picture of FDR looking down at the assembled group. There, the chairman of the Council of Economic Advisers, a University of Chicago economist named Austan Goolsbee, who has long argued that any hidden government subsidies are a recipe for disaster, gave an impassioned performance in which he argued that Fannie and Freddie were villains who needed to be done in.

106 "Mr. President, you've read the comic book and you've seen the movie," Goolsbee began. "You know when you finally catch the super villain and lock him in the special prison that he can never escape from, you do not let him out just because he promises never to do a bad thing again!" According to someone who was present, Obama started cracking up, and said, "Magneto! I've seen that!" The group went back and forth but decided to put forward options rather than endorse a specific plan. Goolsbee says today, "Doing nothing would be better than doing something when the something [wiping out the GSEs] can't be done."

The study required by Dodd-Frank, which Treasury released with HUD in the spring of 2011, described itself as a revelation. "This paper lays out the Administration's plan to reform America's housing finance market to better serve families and function more safely in a world that has changed dramatically since its original pillars were put in place nearly eighty years ago," the authors wrote. It "dramatically transforms the role of government in the housing market."

Actually, all it did was lay out three alternatives. In one, a private system would replace Fannie and Freddie. The FHA would continue to provide narrowly targeted guarantees to very low income borrowers. In the second option, there would be a very minimal government guarantee during good times, but it could be scaled up in a crisis to keep credit flowing. The third option maintained a broader role for the government, but with plenty of private capital in a "first loss" position, meaning that investors would have to lose all their money before taxpayers were on the hook. The white paper offered only options and no

specifics but for one: The goal was to "ultimately wind down"
Fannie and Freddie.

If there was a moment in which something could have been done, it would soon be lost in the increasing partisan divide. After the 2012 elections, Jeb Hensarling, the conservative Republican from Texas, became the chairman of the House Financial Services Committee. When Hensarling talks about Fannie and Freddie, he often uses Peter Wallison and Ed Pinto's analysis. In mid-2013, the House Financial Services Committee passed a bill introduced by Hensarling called the Protecting American Taxpayers and Homeowners Act, or PATH. This bill would wind down Fannie and Freddie within five years. No government guarantee would replace them, and there were no affordable-housing provisions. The bill kept the FHA, but reduced its role to serving only first-time homebuyers and buyers with low to moderate incomes. It is exactly the bill that those who want the government entirely out of the market would like to see passed. It passed strictly along party lines.

But the PATH Act wasn't going anywhere, and not just because of Democrats. "Republicans held their noses and gave him [Hensarling] the votes," says one close observer. "But you never heard of it again because the House leadership said, 'It's not going to the floor.'" Another longtime lobbyist gives Hensarling credit for producing a coherent bill, and says, "He is a true believer. He really does want to end them [Fannie and Freddie]." But as the lobbyist points out, there are plenty of Republicans who take money from the housing industrial complex. The last thing the housing industrial complex wants is to see mortgage rates soar. And so the Realtors, which are among the country's

108   largest political action committees, came out against PATH. "It was anathema to them," says one person who is familiar with the group. There was also the question of what would happen to foreign investors who held Fannie and Freddie securities if the PATH bill passed. "You cannot make overseas investors and Republicans happy in one piece of legislation," a longtime lobbyist says.

Mr. Hedge Fund Goes to Washington

"This can't be right. This is America. It's like I took 80 percent of your house in the financial crisis because you couldn't pay, and then you somehow crawled your way back, and instead of saying, 'Wow, you made it!' I say, 'Now I'm going to take 100 percent.'"
—Bruce Berkowitz, CEO of Fairholme Capital Management

Three days before Hensarling's PATH Act passed the House Financial Services Committee, a $10 billion hedge fund called Perry Capital, which is run by former Goldman Sachs executive and Democratic power player Richard Perry, sued the U.S. government over its handling of the GSEs. The lawsuit was an outgrowth of Perry's investment in Fannie and Freddie, which happened in late 2010, when Perry bought, for 3 cents a share, that supposedly worthless Fannie and Freddie junior preferred stock, the securities that had been originally sold right before conservatorship.

To understand why anyone would invest in Fannie or Freddie at that time—let alone later sue the U.S. government— you have to understand the unique and punitive nature of their bailout. A positive net worth helps the market have confidence in financial institutions like Fannie and Freddie, so they were required to draw money from Treasury to keep their net worth positive. But "net worth" is an accounting concept that factors in estimates of future losses as well as current losses. Fannie and Freddie were required to draw money based on estimates that they would lose billions in the future. These estimates would turn out to be far too high. In addition, while financial institutions in trouble never pay cash dividends, Fannie and Freddie were required to pay a 10 percent dividend back to Treasury on any money they took. This had some perverse consequences. Because the dividend payment further reduced their net worth, they also had to draw additional money from Treasury to fill the hole caused by the dividend payment. According to a FHFA official, around $45 billion of Fannie and Freddie's $187 billion bailout consisted of draws that took money from Treasury only to round-trip it right back to Treasury as a dividend payment. (Other analysts think the figure is lower, around $30 billion.) "It was a complete payday lender situation," says someone close to the situation. "It was like borrowing from a loan shark."

Ultimately, Fannie Mae took $116.1 billion and Freddie Mac $71.3 billion from the U.S. Treasury, a total of $187.4 billion. One analysis done on behalf of a major investor shows that most of the losses were caused by non-cash charges such as provisions for loan losses—losses that never materialized. During the period in which the GSEs lost money, from 2007 to 2011, the provisions for losses exceeded the actual losses by $141.8 billion. Put another way, if Fannie and Freddie had only reported their cash losses, and had kept their deferred tax assets instead of writing them off, they would have lost $64.1 billion, according to this analysis. Considering the amount of equity they held heading into the crisis, their combined equity deficiency would have been only about $10 billion.

But because the GSEs had to pay the dividend on the full amount they drew, Tim Howard would later calculate that Fannie was obligated to make $11.6 billion in dividend payments for every year in the future—more than Fannie had earned in any single year in its history. "Seemingly it was a death sentence," Howard wrote. In a speech in the fall of 2011, Ed DeMarco said Fannie and Freddie "will not be able to earn their way back to a condition that allows them to emerge from conservatorship. In any event, the model on which they were built is broken beyond repair."

When almost everyone was gnashing his teeth about the apparently mounting losses at the GSEs, some investors began to do the math, and they found that Fannie and Freddie weren't doing nearly as poorly as it seemed. One of the first people to call it publicly was an Australian hedge fund manager named John Hempton. In an August 2009 blog post, he noted that the actual cash losses Fannie and Freddie had reported to date were "simply not large enough to have caused problems." After going through filings, he noted that the estimates of future losses were "extremely harsh." Hempton would later call Fannie and Freddie's post-bailout financial report the greatest accounting fraud he'd ever seen. He didn't mean "fraud" in the usual sense of fraud, in which a company understates its losses, thereby making the financial picture look prettier. He thought Fannie and Freddie were *overstating* their losses, thereby making the financial picture look uglier. This was unique, even in the crisis. An analysis done by Fairholme shows that during and after the financial crisis, big banks like JPMorgan Chase and Wells Fargo reserved about the same amount that they eventually took in losses, whereas Fannie and Freddie's provisions for potential losses were much higher than the loan losses they actually incurred.

Some investors also noticed that despite all the rhetoric about killing Fannie and Freddie, when the government put them into conservatorship, Jim Lockhart had said that the goal was to return Fannie and Freddie "to normal business operations" and that "both the preferred and common shareholders have an economic interest in the companies . . . and going forward there may be some value in that interest."

Eventually, if the housing market began to recover, accounting laws would require that the estimated losses that had never materialized be reversed and booked as profits. The deferred tax assets would have to be reinstated, because after all, if the GSEs were profitable again, then the deferred tax assets would have value. The profits would be gigantic. Perry Capital and other major hedge funds began buying up the junior preferred shares, which were still priced near zero. Some of them, like Perry, were funds that had made fortunes betting against, or shorting, subprime mortgages in the run-up to the crisis, which was documented in the book *The Greatest Trade Ever*. Paulson & Co., run by John Paulson, who personally made almost $4 billion from

shorting subprime securities, bought shares. So did a hedge
fund called Claren Road that is majority owned by the Carlyle
Group, the politically connected Washington, D.C.—based asset
management firm.

For a long time, the investors thought Fannie and Freddie
were like normal companies. Conservatorship wasn't supposed
to be forever. Fannie and Freddie required restructuring—they
would need huge amounts of additional capital to get back in
business, and the government would have to revise the terms of
its senior preferred stock—but restructuring is what happens
when companies run into trouble. "We are used to distressed financial companies," one investor says. "We do not shut it down
and vilify the management teams. We figure out what works,
what is salvageable." He points out that when General Motors
declared bankruptcy, its plants didn't all get shut down.

"We expected the political rhetoric," says another investor.
"We thought, 'It's easy for you to say you want to kill them, and
that they are an endless black hole.' But once they were profitable, we thought the rhetoric would change."

What was going on inside of the Treasury at this time is
now the subject of multiple lawsuits. But certainly, people at
Treasury had heard the case for the GSEs' return to profitability. On June 13, 2011, lawyers from the firm Skadden, Arps and
representatives from the Blackstone Group, the sprawling investment corporation run by billionaire Stephen Schwarzman,
which has a group that specializes in restructuring troubled
companies, traveled from New York to see officials at Treasury
to pitch the government on how best to deal with Fannie and
Freddie. According to a presentation they gave, they told

114   Treasury that Fannie and Freddie were showing "improved financial performance and stabilized loss reserves." They urged the Treasury officials to allow Fannie and Freddie to build up fresh capital through their earnings—and to make sure that the investors were paid. As one slide read, "private capital will not make any substantial commitment to a solution in the absence of any likelihood of a meaningful return on equity capital." The translation: Unless the investors got paid for what they owned already, they were certainly not going to contribute to the mortgage market any more of that private capital the government was saying it wanted.

After that, the hedge fund arm of Blackstone, which operates separately from the rest of the group but which had also come to believe that Fannie and Freddie would soon be very profitable, bought some of the outstanding preferred shares too.

There's some evidence that by that time, people at Treasury did know that Fannie and Freddie would return to profitability—and they were worried about it. After all, amid the brewing anti–hedge fund sentiment in Washington, the last thing anyone wanted was to be accused of enabling a payday for wealthy investors from a taxpayer-funded bailout. In December 2010, Jeffrey Goldstein, then the undersecretary for domestic finance at Treasury, wrote an internal memo to Geithner discussing an option that would enable Treasury to "make clear the Administration's commitment to ensure existing common equity holders will not have access to any positive earnings from the GSEs in the future."

Just as investors had predicted, Freddie posted a profit in the fourth quarter of 2011. The next quarter, Fannie did too.

Trading in their outstanding securities went crazy. When the
two companies reported earnings in August 2012, Fannie made
$5 billion, while Freddie made $3 billion. Neither company required money from Treasury anymore.

The Third Amendment
Then, on August 17, 2012, a sleepy summer Friday, Treasury and
the FHFA changed the rules of the game.

Going forward, instead of paying a 10 percent dividend,
Fannie and Freddie would be required to send every penny
they made to Treasury. If everything went to the government,
then there was no value left for investors. Both the common
and the preferred shares plunged in price. Fairholme Capital
Management, which manages around $10 billion on behalf of
some 180,000 individual investors and a few institutions, described it this way in its annual report: "The bureaucrats have
illegally expropriated and de facto nationalized two of the most
valuable companies in the world with apparent impunity."

The government has a justification for what came to be
known as the Third Amendment (because it was the third time
the Treasury had amended the rules governing the bailout.) The
Third Amendment was signed by both Tim Geithner and Ed
DeMarco. Mario Ugoletti, a former Treasury official who joined
DeMarco at FHFA in 2009, would later say in a legal filing that
"institutional and Asian investors" in the GSEs' securities were
worried that there eventually wouldn't be enough money on the
Treasury lifeline given the perilous state of Fannie and Freddie's
finances and the huge dividend payments owed to Treasury. So
it made sense to end the practice of round-tripping, and just

have Fannie and Freddie pay whatever they made, thereby reassuring investors that they'd never run out of funding. (DeMarco won't comment on the Third Amendment, but if he thought that a revitalized Fannie and Freddie would be the worst possible thing for taxpayers, then it's easy to see why he might have endorsed it. Geithner declined to comment.)

It was at this point that Bruce Berkowitz, who runs Fairholme, decided to invest in Fannie and Freddie.

If Perry's investment seemed contrarian, this was, on the face of it, flat-out crazy. But not to Berkowitz, who is what's known as a value investor—someone who seeks out not the next hot technology investment, but rather troubled companies that might have redemption in their futures. He'd been analyzing an investment already. The securities, which had run up in price as hedge funds bought them, plunged to bargain-basement prices. And, he says now, "When I read it [the Third Amendment] I thought there was a typo. This can't be right. This is America. It's like I took 80 percent of your house in the financial crisis because you couldn't pay, and then you somehow crawled your way back, and instead of saying, 'Wow, you made it!' I say, 'Now I'm going to take 100 percent.'"

In Berkowitz's view, the logic was just so obviously flawed: If the government wanted 100 percent of the GSEs, then it should have nationalized them, instead of leaving the preferred and common stock outstanding. Under the law governing conservatorship, the FHFA had a duty to "preserve and conserve" Fannie and Freddie's assets, not just go along with what the Treasury wanted. And the notion that foreign investors were worried seems like an after-the-fact excuse, because in the investors' eyes, it was obvious that Fannie and Freddie were about to become extremely profitable. (A former government official insists that it is "flat-out incorrect" to say that anyone in the government foresaw the coming tidal wave of profits.)

There are a lot of more nefarious theories as to what was really going on. Treasury was worried about Fannie and Freddie being profitable again, because no one wanted to read headlines about hedge funds making fortunes. And the losses helped cement the narrative that the GSE model was a failure, and that Fannie and Freddie must be abolished. "Fannie and Freddie got the concrete life preserver when they were holding the banks' heads up over the water," Tim Howard says. "After they dug themselves out of the hole, Treasury put them back in. That's because they were supposed to be shut down before they became profitable again."

The Piggy Bank

There's also speculation about another factor. The Third Amendment came a year after the huge fight in Congress over raising the debt ceiling. Since that time, battles over spending have become commonplace. The profits generated by Fannie and Freddie, which go straight to Treasury, have at critical times helped buy breathing room, or as Treasury Secretary Jack Lew said in recent congressional testimony, "As a practical matter, it's what has helped us to reduce our overall deficit." One investor jokes bitterly that hedge funds can no longer claim the Greatest Trade Ever: Based on the amount the U.S. government has made from Fannie and Freddie, it's the government that deserves that distinction.

Indeed, Fannie and Freddie's contribution to the U.S. budget has not been small. The Congressional Budget Office has noted that the $83 billion decline in outlays between 2012 and 2013 "resulted primarily from transactions between the Treasury Department and Fannie Mae and Freddie Mac." Thanks to the GSEs' profits, federal spending was underreported by a combined $178 billion in 2013 and 2014, according to a paper by the Heritage Foundation. The authors noted that a new deal struck between Democrats and Republicans came right after Treasury reported the GSEs' 2013 profits. "Undoubtedly, rosy reporting considering short-term improvements in federal spending and the deficit played a role in the decision to increase spending immediately for promised spending reductions in the future," the authors wrote. Not incidentally, there is no accountability for how the profits from Fannie and Freddie are spent; and once the money is spent, it is gone and cannot be used to buffer any losses they might suffer again, or be used to capitalize a new housing finance system.

This is why Berkowitz complains that the government is using "two publicly traded, shareholder-owned companies as a piggy bank." In 2011, before the Third Amendment, the government explicitly funded a continued cut in payroll taxes by having Fannie and Freddie raise their guarantee fees by 10 basis points, or one-tenth of 1 percent. In other words, by government decree, mortgage borrowers paid for the payroll-tax cut.

Suing the government isn't an easy or cheap decision, and the investors initially believed that someone in the government would care about their rights, but Treasury had no interest in hearing from the aggrieved investors, they say. "We tried

to compromise, but there was dead silence," Berkowitz says.
"The same bureaucrats who have repeatedly called for more
private capital to support our housing-finance market view
existing shareholders with outright contempt." But these existing shareholders just happened to be some of the country's
wealthiest investors, and unlike most people, they can afford to
fight. So Perry signed up Theodore Olson, who was the solici-
tor general in the Bush Administration and is now a partner at
the Washington law firm Gibson Dunn, and sued the government. Fairholme was next to file. Eventually, about 20 lawsuits
were filed.

Most plaintiffs agree that the most important issues are
what they allege is the violation of the 2008 law governing conservatorship, which says that Fannie and Freddie are supposed
to be put in a safe and sound condition, and the bailout's third
amendment, which they allege violates the Constitution's Fifth
Amendment: The government cannot confiscate private property without paying for it. In other words, this isn't about the
government's actions in a time of crisis, but rather about the
government's actions after the crisis had passed. "Have you
seen *House of Cards*?" Berkowitz asks, referring to the popular
Netflix show that cynically depicts the rise of a powerfully cor-
rupt president. "It's real!" Many hedge funders invest in other
places around the world, such as Argentina, where governments do things like seize private property with impunity. In
2012, Argentina nationalized assets belonging to a Spanish oil
company called Repsol; in 2014, Argentina agreed to pay Repsol
part of what it was owed in order to bring foreign investment
back to the country. A joke goes: "What's the difference between

the GSEs in the United States and Repsol in Argentina?" The punchline: "Argentina settled."

In Washington, there is a distinct lack of sympathy for the investors and for the argument about their private property rights. Berkowitz recalls complaining to one politically plugged-in person, only to be told to "grow up." There are some in D.C. circles who believe the government only left Fannie and Freddie's common and preferred shares in private hands because it had to do so to avoid putting their debt on the federal budget. Since everyone knew that this was a façade of convenience, the investors should have understood that what they view as their property always belonged to the government. Or as Geithner said in a deposition in an unrelated case, the U.S. government "effectively nationalized" Fannie and Freddie. Add to that the political hatred for the two companies. What makes sense using New York financial logic is borderline insane when you apply a Washington political calculus.

Those who have been around Fannie and Freddie for a long time think the investors were painfully naïve. How could they think this was just another distressed investment when Fannie and Freddie have always been treated differently from other companies? As a former Fannie executive puts it, "Any arrangement that leaves shareholders in place but doesn't allow them to get any value seems like an un-American thing to do. But there are those who would argue that the GSEs are un-American to begin with."

The highly charged, topsy-turvy world of Fannie and Freddie, where those who should be your friends might just be your foes, certainly has been a shock to the investors. One might expect that Republicans would be upset about the government nationalizing an industry, confiscating its profits, and using the money to help a Democratic administration improve its budget deficit. But that is not the case, because the hatred of Fannie and Freddie seems to trump all else. At a recent House Banking Committee event, the conservative economist Peter Wallison was asked if there was any good that could come out of Fannie and Freddie being released from conservatorship. "No," he said. "I'm perfectly happy that government is taking all their profits, because it keeps them from gaining capital. If they had capital there would be tremendous pressure in Congress to release them."

"In a normal world, Republicans would care about the rule of law," says one investor. "But Republicans want to kill Fannie and Freddie, so they want to starve them of capital. Democrats want to keep the system as it is, where the GSEs have been de facto nationalized." Keeping the hedge funds from getting paid crosses party lines.

Defending the
Common Man

"Fannie and Freddie provide services that are absolutely essential to the American way of life . . . No one does it better."
—Bruce Berkowitz, CEO of Fairholme Capital Management

Thus far, the investors seem to be losing their battle in the courts. In the fall of 2014, Judge Royce Lamberth dismissed Perry Capital's suit in the D.C. District Court. Lamberth is an old-school Republican, and the investors thought they had a good shot, but his decision was short, sweeping, and shocking to the investors. One provision in the Housing Economic Recovery Act reads, "No court may take any action to restrain or affect the exercise of powers or functions of the Director as a conservator or a receiver." And so, in essence, Lamberth said that the government could do whatever it wanted. "It is understandable for the Third Amendment, which sweeps nearly all GSE profits to Treasury, to raise eyebrows, or even engender a

feeling of discomfort," he wrote. "But any sense of unease over
the defendants' [i.e., the government's] conduct is not enough
to overcome the plain meaning of HERA's text."Both the common and preferred shares plunged in value.

The decision was a momentous one, and it was followed by
Judge Robert Pratt's decision to dismiss Continental Western's
case in Iowa, mainly on procedural grounds: Pratt argued that
the case was too similar to the one Lamberth had just dismissed.
Perry is appealing Lamberth's decision. In the meantime, other
cases continue, and they will likely take years to resolve. Most
recently, Judge Margaret Sweeney has allowed discovery to pro-
ceed in the case Fairholme brought in the U.S. Court of Federal
Claims. Investors are hoping discovery will yield a trove of
damaging documents. "The case could put additional heat on
the White House, which is at risk of having to disgorge embar-
rassing internal communications that, in some scenarios, might
be cast by critics as the equivalent of a scandal," wrote a longtime GSE analyst named Chuck Gabriel. The government has
fought like mad to keep documents private, arguing that any
disclosure "could literally affect interest rates," as a lawyer for
the Department of Justice said in a recent hearing. "These documents [could] have a devastating effect on our economy."

The investors aren't without allies, who are capable of making a lot of noise about what they also see as the government's
above-the-law behavior. The libertarian economist Mark
Calabria, the former Shelby staffer who worked on the bills
that eventually became the Housing and Economic Recovery
Act of 2008, and Michael Krimminger, who spent 20 years at
the Federal Deposit Insurance Corporation, most recently as the

general counsel, wrote in the American Banker that "the perpetual conservatorships and Treasury sweeps are a violation of every principle of insolvency law."

While the lawsuits represent a frontal assault by the investors, the more important drama might be behind the scenes. Some investors say that they view the lawsuits merely as a wedge to force the door open to what they really want: a recapitalized, albeit heavily reformed, version of Fannie and Freddie, which, they argue, is the right solution for the housing market—as well as one that would increase the value of their stock. This, of course, is precisely what the administration has said it does not want.

In the spring of 2014, the hedge fund manager and activist investor Bill Ackman announced that his fund, Pershing Square, had bought 13 percent of the remaining 20 percent of the GSEs' common stock. Pershing Square also sued the government. But the purchase of common stock is essentially an all-in bet that Fannie and Freddie will be revitalized in some way. In a presentation he called "It's Time to Get Off Our Fannie," Ackman laid out a plan for the future of the housing finance system, essentially calling for the return of Fannie and Freddie. A new and improved version, yes, but Fannie and Freddie, better capitalized, better regulated, and required to stick to one business: guaranteeing the credit risk on mortgages. Ackman argues that the real loss numbers show that had Fannie and Freddie stuck to that core business, they would have survived the crisis, even with their thin layer of capital.

Fairholme has also purchased some of the common stock, and Berkowitz is in complete agreement: Given the things that we as a society seem to want, like a 30-year fixed-rate mortgage that is available in good times and bad, there is no good alternative to the GSEs. "Our investment was predicated on a simple thesis: there are no substitutes. Fannie and Freddie provide services that are absolutely essential to the American way of life," he wrote in the fund's annual report. "They help make the popular 30-year fixed-rate mortgage available and affordable. They provide liquidity and stability to the nation's housing finance system—during good and, especially, in bad times. No one does it better." He compares housing reform to Obamacare. "Obama can get a do-over when he says, 'You can keep your insurance!' 'Oops, you can't keep your insurance!'" he says. "But you cannot mess up the plumbing of housing finance. If you do, within two weeks, credit will totally dry up. No one will be able to get a mortgage."

There is disagreement among investors on many details of how a plan would work. But there's a general consensus about this. If you want to keep long-term fixed-rate mortgages widely available at nationally uniform rates, there is simply no way to fund a replacement housing-finance system without using the profits generated by Fannie and Freddie, and without keeping some kind of strong backstop that explicitly (in which case the companies would pay a fee to the government) or implicitly (as the old system worked) involves the government. There are several reasons for this. Many big bond investors do not like credit risk. They are not equipped to analyze whether or not millions of homeowners will pay their mortgages; in fact, the pension funds and others who give them money to invest often don't allow them to take credit risk. Another is that the American

126   mortgage business is so mammoth. There are about $5 trillion of Fannie and Freddie securities outstanding now. If you assume that they need to be backed by 5 percent capital, then you need $250 billion. To put that in context, Ackman calculated in his presentation that the four largest U.S. banks together had an equity market value of $844 billion; the total proceeds from the approximately 1,500 initial public offerings in the U.S. over the last decade was $386 billion. The total equity value of all private mortgage insurers today is a mere $10 billion—a drop in the ocean. What private-market participant is going to invest in a new system given the untested nature of it? Nor is a high return to investors commensurate with low mortgage rates.

Not incidentally, there's an argument, which is valid at least in a short-term sense, that recapitalizing a reformed Fannie and Freddie is also the outcome that is in taxpayers' best interest. Treasury has the right to own almost 80 percent of Fannie and Freddie, and if they are resuscitated and taken public again, that stake could be worth hundreds of billions of dollars, making Fannie and Freddie far and away the most successful bailout in history and putting substantial new resources into the federal treasury. Which all helps explain why Ackman can say, with a straight face, "We're defending the common man."

"It's a glorious win for everyone," says Berkowitz. "I don't understand why no one will make any compromises. Everyone wins and the country moves on."

No End in Sight

"If you think about homeownership as the major way the middle class—at least since World War II—has built assets, it also is part of our concern about inequality, economic growth, and social harmony."
—Ellen Seidman, Director of the Office of Thrift Supervision, 1997–2001

In early 2014, just after investors had begun to sue, the White House was finally able to replace Ed DeMarco as the acting head of Fannie and Freddie's conservator. This happened after Democrats, frustrated by their inability to confirm nominees, took the dramatic step of eliminating filibusters for most of the president's nominations. This allowed the administration to appoint Mel Watt, a gracious, charming, liberal Democratic former congressman from North Carolina and a longtime evangelist for homeownership.

DeMarco took a position at the Milken Institute, a pro-market think tank run by former junk-bond king Michael

Milken. (Right around that time, Milken wrote an op-ed for the *Wall Street Journal* in which he argued that subsidized mortgages create nothing good. "Investments in quality education and improved health will do more to accelerate economic growth than excessive housing incentives," he wrote.) A few months later, DeMarco gave a speech at the Richmond Federal Reserve. "Restoring Fannie Mae and Freddie Mac is not the solution," he said. "They failed and their business model failed. Going backwards to an obviously failed model cannot be dressed up with some promise of higher capital or explicit rather than implicit guarantees."

Despite the fight between DeMarco and the administration over principal reduction, the appointment of Watt seemed like an odd lurch, given that based on everything that had been said publicly, DeMarco and the White House seemed to agree on a critical issue: the need to kill Fannie and Freddie. There were some in the administration, particularly on the economics team, who were opposed to Watt's nomination for that reason. "It sent a signal that we were jerking this to the left," says a former official. And although Watt, at least initially, would not be as liberal as some wanted, and he is still new in his role, it's safe to say that some of what happened next would never have happened under Ed DeMarco. "He's certainly not focused on shrinking their footprint," Mark Calabria told the *American Banker*. "Almost everything he has done makes it more likely that the status quo continues."

Watt walked into a tough situation, even beyond the political stew over the eventual fate of his wards. Almost seven years of government control over every aspect of their operations

were and are taking a toll on Fannie and Freddie, even beyond
the people problems you'd expect when employees don't know
if their company will exist in a few years. "It is running a low-
grade fever all the time," says one employee. Although the FHFA,
Fannie and Freddie's regulator, says that it has "delegated" to the
CEOs and boards "responsibility for much of the day-to-day
operations," this person claims that the FHFA is doing what a
government agency usually does, which is to try to impose systems that will eliminate the exercise of human judgment. This
is a problem, because huge, fast-moving markets like the mortgage market require the constant exercise of human judgment.
"If the country wants to have this function, you want it to be
nimble, because that's what financial markets require. We are
not nimble," this employee says.

"It [conservatorship] has been structured as purgatory,"
says a former Fannie executive. "Conservatorship is a misno-
mer. You conserve in anticipation of something. There has been
no something." He adds: "The fact folks miss is that people who
have neutered are negotiating billion-dollar transactions with
these big banks."

To those who have been on the inside, conservatorship
may be sustainable, but it is far from ideal. "GSE Island" is how
one former FHFA employee describes his view of life inside the
agency, because he says the FHFA, in its policies and focus, is so
different from other regulators. Under conservatorship, it has
been impossible for either FHFA or the companies to make long-
term decisions, like those about strategic investments, or per-
sonnel. He also claims that FHFA, which is intimately involved
in the day-to-day activities of Fannie and Freddie, can at times

130   be hindered by a lack of experience regulating financial institu-
        tions, combined with an odd mixture of inherited subservience
        and passive-aggressiveness toward Fannie and Freddie left over
        from the old days of OFHEO, its predecessor agency. He says
        he'd hear longtime FHFA employees say, "Well, they're just too
        big to regulate."

        In addition to the existential issues, Watt also had to cope
        with short-term pressure to do something, anything, to help fix
        a still-struggling housing market. The overall homeownership
        rate is down to 64 percent—not incidentally, about the same
        level as in the early 1980s at the advent of securitization. The
        rate has fallen particularly steeply in minority communities.
        New home construction and new home-purchase mortgages are
        lagging badly. "While housing usually leads the country out of
        recession, this time it is an anchor," Jonathan Weisman wrote in
        the *New York Times*.

        The crisis and the slow recovery have not done much to
        affect the country's stated commitment to homeownership. In
        some ways, the fragile economic times have only intensified it.
        "I think it's important to understand this is not some abstract
        problem," said Ellen Seidman, the former director of the Office
        of Thrift Supervision in the Clinton Administration, at a re-
        cent panel at the Urban Institute. "It relates to the question of
        how we will house an America in which many more families will
        reach their 30s and 40s burdened with student debt, with less
        certain and lower incomes, and less family financial support
        than was the case for the last two generations."

        Policy makers and politicians across the board, from
        Federal Reserve Chair Janet Yellen to President Obama, have

started complaining about credit standards being too tight.
This criticism would have been unimaginable only a few short
years ago when memories of the crisis were visceral. The pen-
dulum swung with astonishing speed, and Fannie and Freddie
are at the heart of the complaints. Partly because they have
no capital with which to absorb losses, since 2008 Fannie and
Freddie have purchased mortgages made to people with almost pristine credit. According to the National Community
Reinvestment Coalition, in 2012 Fannie and Freddie would only
purchase mortgages made to people with credit scores of over
750, but barely one in five households in the country has a mark
that high. This drastically limits the number of people who can
get mortgages. Critics say, just as they did before the crisis, that
Fannie and Freddie should be taking more risk so more people
have the chance to become homeowners.

And without GSE backing, banks have shown very little
interest in lending to American homeowners, even ones with
very high credit scores, despite DeMarco's having tried to entice
private capital into the housing market by raising guarantee
fees. Last year, there were fewer than $10 billion of private-
label securities sold, compared to a peak of over $1 trillion before
the crisis. "Everyone seems to think when it gets back to normal, the banks will come back in," says a former Fannie lobbyist
who now works for one of the big banks. "But we are seven years
post-crisis. I don't see an end in sight. I think we're in this for
quite some time." "Everyone says that if we increase guarantee
fees enough, private capital will come back in," David Min says.
"But there is no evidence that will happen. Literally, there is
zero evidence."

Fixing the Roof

"These organizations are grossly undercapitalized and represent one heck of a risk to the taxpayers if something goes wrong."
—Bruce Poliquin, Republican Representative of Maine

Shortly after Mel Watt was sworn in as the new director of FHFA in early 2014, he put a hold on the steady increases in guarantee fees and the higher charges for riskier loans that Ed DeMarco had instituted. If private capital wasn't coming back in, it was counterproductive to keep pushing up the guarantee fees. Watt was also very clear about something else: Unlike DeMarco, he was not going to attempt to make policy. That was Congress's job.

In 2013, two senators, Democrat Mark Warner of Virginia and Republican Bob Corker of Tennessee, had begun working on an alternative to the idea of totally eliminating the government from the market. Their plan, which they introduced in the summer of 2013, had five Republican and four Democratic co-sponsors. In essence, it would have abolished Fannie and Freddie over five years and replaced them with a system of private insurers that had to be able to absorb 10 percent of any losses before a government guarantee would kick in. The new insurers would pay an explicit fee to the government in exchange for the guarantee. All of Fannie's and Freddie's functionality—their securitization technology and their infrastructure that handles the acquisition of mortgages—would be recreated as platforms that any private-market participant could use.

The Corker-Warner plan would have accomplished a critical political goal: It would have killed Fannie and Freddie. But there was an element of absurdity to it, in that the plan would have torn everything down just to rebuild a system that, in a key way, would have been similar to what we had. The government, meaning taxpayers, would still be on the hook.

Back in 2012, Jim Millstein, a longtime bankruptcy expert who served as the Treasury's chief restructuring officer during the crisis, had devised his own plan. Millstein's plan also keeps a government backstop, along with Fannie and Freddie's functionality. But one huge difference is that the Corker-Warner plan satisfied the need for what Millstein has called "the ritual slaughter" of Fannie and Freddie, whereas Millstein's plan would use their profits and existing infrastructure as the basis for a new system. Indeed, Millstein says he actually laid out his plan to Corker. After about 45 minutes, Corker looked at him and said, "So Fannie and Freddie survive?" Millstein explained that he didn't think it was realistic to kill them off. "They sit in the middle of an $11 trillion mortgage credit market, and are more than half of it," he recalls saying. "For 80 million American

134   families, their homes are their most important asset. You can-
       not kill Fannie and Freddie without putting the value of 80 mil-
       lion homes at risk." Corker said that he simply couldn't sell a
       plan to his caucus that didn't abolish Fannie and Freddie.

       It might seem shocking that any Republicans would sign
       on to a system that kept any kind of government guarantee. But
       there is widespread agreement among policy makers on at least
       this element of investors' argument, which is that you cannot
       keep a cheap, long-term, fixed-rate mortgage available to the
       wide swath of Americans through big economic ups and downs
       without some sort of government backstop. There is a reason no
       other country has such a product. For all the supposed ideological
       purity in today's Washington, no politician wants to be respon-
       sible for the loss of something Americans have come to see as
       a right. Indeed, despite Alan Greenspan's admonition years ago
       that many Americans would do better with adjustable-rate mort-
       gages, in November 2014 a stunning 87 percent of Americans
       who took out a mortgage to buy a house chose a 30-year fixed-
       rate mortgage, according to data from the Urban Institute.

       Inside the administration, Gene Sperling, the director of the
       National Economic Council, was pushing reform the most. He'd
       worked in the Clinton Administration, and he used to paraphrase
       Clinton quoting JFK: "The best time to fix the roof is when the
       sun is shining." He argued to President Obama that fixing Fannie
       and Freddie was part of fixing the crisis, and if they didn't do it,
       they'd have left a huge hole. He'd say to skeptics: "How can you
       think the status quo is okay? The status quo is absurd!"

Through a group run by Sperling, the administration worked closely with Corker and Warner to make the bill acceptable to President Obama. He never specifically endorsed it, but in a speech that August in Phoenix, he said that it embodies the "four core principles for what I believe reform should look like," the first being that "private capital should take a bigger role in the mortgage market." He also reiterated that Fannie and Freddie must die. "It was 'heads we win, tails you lose,'" he said, referring to the way Fannie and Freddie used to operate. "And it was wrong."

By the spring of 2014, an amended version of the bill had passed the Senate Banking Committee with a bipartisan vote of 13 to 9. But the bill had enemies right off the bat. The investors didn't like it because their only hope for making money would be the lawsuits; they would not have any stake in the new system. They lobbied against the bill in ways that were mostly covert. "The litigants were not helpful," says a former Obama Administration official. "What really hurt about it was, there would be a slight bit of deference with Congress that we knew what we were doing, but then members would be at a fundraiser, and a billionaire would tell them that getting rid of Fannie and Freddie is a terrible idea." Hard-core ideological conservatives didn't like the bill because it retained a heavy government role in the market. Small lenders were wary because they thought that without Fannie and Freddie to sell their mortgages to, the big banks would take over the market and push them out.

But the most surprising, and the strongest, opposition came from some progressive groups, most notably John Taylor's National Community Reinvestment Coalition. Supporters were

shocked, because the bill did assess fees for the purpose of establishing funds for affordable housing. What more could progressives want? But there were no specific requirements that
new insurers had to serve a broad cross section of the American
market—and no affordable-housing goals. As a result, it was un-
likely that the system would make stronger borrowers subsidize
weaker borrowers, as happened in the old Fannie and Freddie
days. In Taylor's view, while very low income renters would be
helped by the specifically dedicated funds, those homebuyers
with slightly weaker credit in less desirable neighborhoods who
just needed access to what he calls "market level" loans would
be at the mercy of the private lenders who Taylor argues created
the crisis in the first place.

The National Community Reinvestment Coalition put
its member organizations around the country to work per-
suading progressive senators, including Sherrod Brown, Jeff
Merkley, and Elizabeth Warren, the firebrand Democrat from
Massachusetts, to vote against the bill. Eventually, a group of
six senators agreed to vote against the bill unless they were satisfied with its affordable-housing language. "What we tried to
impart to senators was, 'This is the way out.' You join in the middle class when you get a home, an asset that grows along with
your earned income, and that gets the tax laws working in your
favor," Taylor recalls. "People [in this income bracket] don't have
401(k)s or stock market income and now the private sector is
buying up homes and raising rents in low- to moderate-income
areas." Taylor continues: "Bernanke [Ben Bernanke, the former
Federal Reserve chairman] wrote a paper arguing that people
should rent, because we focus too much on homeownership in

this country. I call his paper 'Let Them Eat Rent.'" (Bernanke's
paper advocated that some foreclosed homes be converted to
rental properties in order to help restore the health of the housing market.)

The bill never made it to the Senate floor, because Majority
Leader Harry Reid said he would not move the bill if it split the
Democrats. This wasn't surprising, given that in 2013, when
Obama made his remarks about Fannie and Freddie in Phoenix,
Reid said this to a local radio station: "He [Obama] says he
wants to get rid of [Fannie and Freddie]. We've got to be very,
very careful doing that. I have no problem looking at them, re-
vamping. But I think getting rid of them is not the right thing
to do." And, despite the serious involvement of people like
Sperling and Shaun Donovan, then the secretary of HUD, there
was chatter among the progressive Democrats, says one person
who worked on the bill, that it did not have the enthusiastic
support of the rest of the White House political and legisla-
tive operation. It's not clear that the White House ever threw
its weight behind the bill. "The administration did not secure a
single Democratic vote," says one staffer. "If it were that important, the president would have pushed it. He did not even call
any of the Democrats."

The administration also had unintentionally undermined
itself by appointing Mel Watt, a man deeply trusted by housing groups on the left. "There is a school of thought that there
is nothing that could possibly get congressional approval
that would serve low-and middle-income people better than
conservatorship under Mel Watt," says another participant in
the drafting.

Thus far, Mel Watt has done many things that progressives want. What he has not done is agree to principal forgiveness on the remaining underwater mortgages, despite a blasting from Elizabeth Warren on the topic. Taken individually, Watt's steps don't mean much, but looked at in entirety, they amount to a significant departure from DeMarco's policies. Last fall, FHFA reduced the down-payment requirement on loans Fannie and Freddie would buy from 5 percent to 3 percent. More recently, the FHFA directed Fannie and Freddie to begin sending a small percentage—4.2 basis points, or .042 percent—of the value of new loans they guarantee to affordable-housing trust funds that are dedicated to low-income borrowers and renters. Those payments had been suspended by DeMarco under the conservatorship. Watt terminated the suspension. The amount put into the funds is expected to be as much as $500 million a year.

There is some pushback on this. In a hearing in early 2015, Republican lawmakers repeatedly asked how funding the affordable-housing trust funds could make sense given the GSEs' lack of capital. They pointed out that with $3.3 trillion in outstanding guarantees and $9.5 billion in capital, Fannie Mae is currently leveraged at 341 to 1, and with $2.2 trillion in outstanding guarantees and $13 billion in capital, Freddie Mac is leveraged at 170 to 1. That compares to a maximum leverage ratio of about 20 to 1 for the biggest banks that is supposed to go into effect by 2018. "These organizations are grossly undercapitalized and represent one heck of a risk to the taxpayers if something goes wrong," said Maine's Republican Representative Bruce Poliquin in the hearing. He then asked Mel Watt if he agreed.

"I have two responses to it. I wasn't even there when it [the
agreement to send every penny to Treasury] was created. So I
am living under that. I can't change it," said Watt. "But the second response is, you all can change that. Everything that you
just talked about you can change by doing GSE reform."

Shaky Ground

"Fannie and Freddie play an integral role in ensuring that America's housing market is accessible to all Americans equally and this must be preserved."
—"Tim Howard"

Back when everyone was talking about abolishing Fannie and Freddie, former Fannie CEO Franklin Raines would say privately: "They will be around a lot longer than anyone thinks. Give it ten years or so, and maybe we'll name them Bob and Tom, instead of Fannie and Freddie, but there they will be."

At a Goldman Sachs conference on housing finance in early 2015, Michael Stegman, the Treasury official who is now in charge of housing finance, spoke. He knew that many of the hedge funders who had invested in Fannie and Freddie securities were in the crowd. He said that the administration "believes that private capital should be at the center of the housing finance system." And he reiterated that Fannie and Freddie had to die. "The critical flaws in the legacy system that allowed private shareholders and senior employees of the GSEs to reap substantial profits while leaving taxpayers to shoulder enormous losses cannot be fixed by a regulator or conservator because they are intrinsic to the GSEs' congressional charters," he said.

The rhetoric is still tough, but by the spring of 2015, the administration's lack of coherent action was beginning to increase odds that Raines might be right. What seemed inconceivable and horrifying in the wake of the crisis of 2008—that we would ever have anything like Fannie and Freddie again—has come to seem, if not inevitable, then at least like an idea that can be raised in polite company. "I've repeatedly said since 2009 that the further in time we get from the crisis, the greater the probability that Fannie Mae and Freddie Mac would survive in some form," wrote the Cato Institute economist and former HUD deputy assistant secretary Mark Calabria in a blog post in February 2015. "Such looks like an ever-increasing likelihood."

A surprising number of people have begun to argue, in essence, better the devil you sort of know. If a new system is going to look somewhat like the old Fannie and Freddie anyway, with a broad government backstop, why would you start from scratch instead of fixing what we have? The idea, which is precisely along the lines of what investors want, is that if Fannie and Freddie have much higher capital levels, more competent regulation, maybe an explicit guarantee for which they pay the government, and no portfolio business, then you have fixed many of the problems with the business model. Joshua Rosner, the independent analyst who has long been critical of Fannie and Freddie, now says that all of this plus regulating the GSEs as utilities—with caps on their rates of return—is better than the alternatives. Franklin Raines has his own idea, which is to have Fannie and Freddie become cooperatives that are owned by homeowners, much as big insurance cooperatives like State Farm are owned by policyholders. Former Fannie CFO Tim Howard (who is consulting for Fairholme) recently wrote in a paper: "Treasury's insistence on 'killing the ghosts' of two companies that no longer exist is the single biggest impediment to mortgage reform. Treasury needs to accept the fact that they have beaten the Fannie Mae and Freddie Mac they once found so objectionable, put that fight behind them, and turn their attention to helping to build a mortgage finance system for the twenty-first century."

While Fannie and Freddie still can't lobby on their own behalf, they almost don't need to anymore. A case in point came in late 2014 when the Congressional Budget Office issued a report, the gist of which was that getting rid of Fannie and Freddie would be a great idea. The CBO argued that mortgage rates would increase, at most, 60 basis points from where they are today, and housing prices might fall 2.5 percent. The *Wall Street Journal*'s editorial page seized upon the report. "The housing lobby likes to pretend that 30-year fixed-rate mortgages would hardly exist without a federal guarantee, or would only be available to borrowers at extremely high prices. CBO's report makes it much tougher to sell that fairy tale."

Unlike two decades ago, Fannie people didn't call the CBO "economic pencil brains." But similar language came from an ardently pro—Fannie and Freddie blogger who calls himself Tim

Howard, but isn't, and who has offered a $1 million reward to anyone with information about the "government's lawless attempted seizure" of Fannie and Freddie. He immediately responded to the CBO report with a post saying: "Our opponents are not going to surrender quietly. Just as we warned, we see a desperate, intensive last gasp attempt to salvage their goal of eliminating Fannie and Freddie. . . . The only conclusion any sane reader could draw from the report is that it would be beyond reckless to abandon a system that has worked so well for over 80 years in exchange for one of the untested schemes in the report. The reality is that private capital has a long sordid disastrous history in the secondary mortgage market, they have never been successful at it. Their involvement always leads to predatory style lending, high risk business practices and always has ended in complete collapse."

The real Tim Howard says he doesn't have any involvement in the fake Tim Howard's efforts, but that "people were screaming into the wind without any idea how to identify an objective and mount a campaign to get it done. Now, it's starting to happen."

There certainly is a pro—Fannie and Freddie campaign. Its broad thrust is to pressure Mel Watt to bring Fannie and Freddie out of conservatorship using his administrative powers, a path that would begin by allowing them to keep their earnings, instead of sending everything to the Treasury. That's of course what the investors want, because it would probably cause the price of their Fannie and Freddie stocks to rise significantly. But the pressure isn't just coming from investors. The Community Mortgage Lenders of America, a local bankers' group, also wants Watt to end conservatorship. "What is the point of having the

GSEs generate large profits if this does not make the GSEs more financially stable, thereby enhancing the safety and soundness of the mortgage marketplace?" the group asks. Recently, Wade Henderson, president and CEO of the Leadership Conference on Civil and Human Rights, and Milton Rosado, national president of the Labor Council for Latin American Advancement, wrote their own letter to Watt. "In order to ensure the best path forward for increasing homeownership in the communities we represent, we believe it is vital to initiate serious discussions about unwinding the conservatorship and allowing Fannie and Freddie to begin rebuilding their capital," Henderson and Rosado wrote. "Fannie and Freddie can be fixed; discarding them in entirety would be a colossal mistake."

But the fight is by no means over. At least publicly, the administration has not budged from its position that Fannie and Freddie must die. There is also pressure on Watt from another front. In March 2015, a group of senators, including Bob Corker, sent Watt a letter urging him to open up the new platform Fannie and Freddie are building to turn mortgages into securities to private-sector participants. Although the senators went out of their way to say that this would be good for small and mid-sized lenders, in Rosner's view it is an effort to begin to hand over what was the GSEs' market to the nation's biggest banks. That is problematic for two reasons. The first is that there would be a blurred line between the business of originating mortgages and that of guaranteeing mortgages, a line that Rosner argues is critical if you want the guarantors to support the housing market in troubled times when originators are pulling back. The second is that it would negate the efforts in the Dodd-Frank financial

reform bill to allow big banks to fail, because if they are both
the front-end and back-end machinery of the mortgage market,
then of course they cannot be allowed to fail (even if the source
of the problem was, say, derivatives, not housing). And all the
political power, and pressure, of homeownership that once ac-
crued to the GSEs will now solely accrue to the big banks.

Watt, for his part, continues to maintain that the future
of Fannie and Freddie should be decided by Congress. ("Watt
is never off script," says one maybe overly optimistic investor.
"But he could be a great Trojan Horse, and just one day, it'll be,
boom! We're taking them out.")

In other words, Fannie and Freddie are still a battleground,
as they have always been, and the battle is being fought in covert
ways, as it always has been.

Is there a "right" outcome? Maybe in an ideal world, yes.
There was supposed to be a silver lining to the financial crisis.
For a short time after 2008, there was a brief moment when it
looked as if there were going to be a grand reassessment of the
primacy of homeownership in American life. "It was as if we hit
PAUSE, and could reset everything," Dan Mudd, Fannie's former
CEO, says. "But," he adds, "the moment is lost."

Indeed, neither of the solutions that look the likeliest right
now—handing the market to the banks, or bringing back a version of Fannie and Freddie—does anything to rethink the cult
of homeownership. While increasing the power and the size
of the banks certainly has its risks, reformed GSEs obviously
have their risks too. Critics like Austan Goolsbee, former chairman of the Council of Economic Advisers under Obama, argue
that whatever safeguards you put in, the flawed nature of the

structure—having any kind of government subsidy that isn't fully paid for—means it will inevitably go bad. "They might not be named Fannie and Freddie, but the problem is the problem, and the losses will come again," says Goolsbee. "In which case, shame on us. We just lived this and we knew how to prevent it." He argues that even if the government guarantee is priced appropriately initially, meaning that it covers the risk, the pricing will inevitably become politicized by the housing industrial complex. And it may not be possible to price the risk appropriately. If you do, those who can opt out will do so, leaving the weaker credits to the government, which actually magnifies the problem.

"If what happens is, we all forget and three years from now we basically reinvent the old Fannie and Freddie with a slightly different structure and new rhetoric about regulation, then this whole thing will have been a huge failure," Larry Summers says.

And there are many reasons we should have started from scratch. This system we live with was established in the 1930s, which was a very different time. Why do we need long-term fixed-rate mortgages in a world where the work force of the future is going to change jobs and move every three to five years? Why do we even need homeownership? Shouldn't it be a world of renters? If what we need is energy-efficient multifamily housing for an urbanized world, what are we doing subsidizing the construction of ever-larger single-family homes? Even more, if what we want to subsidize is homeownership, why not limit government backing to first-time homebuyers, and exclude refinancings, or at least cash-out refinancings? Oh, and don't cheap mortgages just make homes more expensive?

Perhaps even more important, we live in a world of limited
resources. Why should we put the government's weight behind homeownership, of all things? Why not subsidize medi-
cal research, for instance? "Housing for housing's sake—the
proverbial 'American Dream'—is an ill-considered and, as we
learned the very hard way, a costly call," Karen Shaw Petrou,
the co-founder and managing partner of research firm Federal
Financial Analytics, wrote recently.

But maybe this line of thinking was hopelessly hyper-
rational. We are trapped by a need to maintain homeownership,
because our economy literally depends on it. You cannot just hit
RESET without a level of financial pain the country may not be
able to endure. "Whether you like the GSEs or not, it's about 80
years too late to have that discussion," says a Fannie employee.
"We have already built an economy around this and used this to
invest in leveling the effects of capitalism. The idea of unwinding it all is crazy." Maybe we could have, and should have, chosen
jobs, or healthcare, but we didn't. We chose housing.

If there's still a silver lining, it may be that today's younger
generations are very different from the home-buying popula-
tions of the second half of the 1990s. They are far more diverse,
racially and culturally. They are more urban. And they are more
mobile. The shape of the housing market will ultimately be dic-
tated not just by what is available to these generations, but also
by the choices they make.

In the meantime, though, Fannie Mae and Freddie Mac are
a huge, consequential, and fundamentally unstable part of the
American economic system, one that also has political ramifications. Even if the courts strike down all the investors' lawsuits,

148   that is ultimately a Pyrrhic victory for the government if there
      is still no resolution about the structure of the housing market.
      Because most American homeowners don't know that they are
      in an intimate financial relationship with these enormous com-
      panies, it's left to the interest groups and the politicians to fight
      out their future in private, and thus far that hasn't produced
      happy results. The two companies are, for financial institutions,
      severely undercapitalized. At the moment they are being used as
      cash cows to make the federal deficit appear smaller than it re-
      ally is. But if market conditions, including the Federal Reserve's
      sale of the agency securities it owns, destabilize them, they
      don't have a cushion, and the effects on the American home-
      owner—and even on U.S. foreign relations, because of the large
      financial interests of other major world powers in Fannie and
      Freddie's debt—could be devastating. The American housing
      market must be placed on firmer ground. If we simply cannot
      move away from the cult of homeownership right now, then let's
      fix what we have.

FURTHER READINGS

For a look at many of the causes and key players that led to the 2008 financial crisis, see my previous book, written with Joe Nocera. *All the Devils Are Here: The Hidden History of the Financial Crisis* (Portfolio, 2010).

For a detailed history of Fannie Mae that explains the company's controversial origins, written by *Wall Street Journal* reporter James R. Hagerty: *The Fateful History of Fannie Mae: New Deal Birth to Mortgage Crisis Fall* (The History Press, 2012).

On the Brink: Inside the Race to Stop the Collapse of the Global Financial System, by Henry Paulson (Business Plus, 2010). The former Treasury Secretary's memoir of coping with the 2008 financial crisis, which begins with the takeover of Fannie and Freddie.

Hidden in Plain Sight: What Really Caused the World's Worst Financial Crisis and Why It Could Happen Again, by Peter Wallison (Encounter Books, 2015). Wallison, a scholar at the American Enterprise Institute, argues that the affordable-housing goals that Congress required the GSEs to fulfill caused the financial crisis.

Sarah Lehman Quinn's 2010 dissertation at the University of California, Berkeley, "Government Policy, Housing, and the Origins of Securitization, 1780–1968," explains how federal housing policy has and hasn't aligned with the federal government's involvement in housing finance since the earliest days of the United States. You can read it here: https://escholarship. org/uc/item/7sq3f6xk

In a March 2015 Federal Reserve Bank of New York staff report, four economists, W. Scott Frame, Andreas Fuster, Joseph Tracy, and James Vickery, analyze the decision to put Fannie and Freddie into conservatorship. It is called "The Rescue of Fannie Mae and Freddie Mac," and you can read it here: http://www.newyorkfed.org/research/staff_reports/sr719.pdf

The Congressional Budget Office analyzes the various alternatives for a housing finance system in a 2014 report, "Transitioning to Alternative Structures for Housing Finance": https://www.cbo.gov/publication/49765

"Housing Finance System: A Framework for Assessing Potential Changes," October 2014. The U.S. Government Accountability Office weighs in on

the challenges facing the housing finance system: http://www.gao.gov/
products/GAO-15-131

"Assessing the Public Costs and Benefits of Fannie Mae and Freddie Mac."
The Congressional Budget Office issued a 1996 report that analyzed
the amount of the subsidy Fannie Mae and Freddie Mac received via the
government's implicit guarantee of their debt and mortgage-backed
securities. http://catalog.hathitrust.org/Record/011346201

*The Mortgage Wars: Inside Fannie Mae, Big-Money Politics, and the Collapse of
the American Dream*, by Tim Howard (McGraw-Hill, 2013). The former chief
financial officer of Fannie Mae offers his version of events.

*Guaranteed to Fail: Fannie Mae, Freddie Mac, and the Debacle of Mortgage
Finance*, by Viral V. Acharya, Matthew Richardson, Stijn van Nieuwerburgh,
and Lawrence J. White (Princeton University Press, 2011). Four economists
offer an academic view of the history of the GSEs and the causes of the crisis.

"Housing in the New Millennium: A Home Without Equity is Just a Rental
with Debt." In 2001, independent research analyst Joshua Rosner pointed
out the brewing danger in the housing market long before the financial
crisis erupted. http://papers.ssrn.com/sol3/papers.cfm?abstract_id=1162456

11 **"Those of us who have
looked"**: "Greenspan Concedes
Error on Regulation," by Edmund L.
Andrews, *New York Times,* October
23, 2008. http://www.nytimes.
com/2008/10/24/business/
economy/24panel.html

19 **"one of the biggest potential
paydays in history"**: "Westhus
Reaping Fannie Windfall to Rival Big
Short: Mortgages," by Jody Shenn,
Bloomberg, March 10, 2014. http://
www.bloomberg.com/news/arti-
cles/2014-03-10/westhus-reaping-
fannie-windfall-to-rival-big-short-
mortgages

21 **"suggesting that they might
together"**: *On the Brink: Inside the
Race to Stop the Collapse of the Global
Financial System,* by Henry Paulson
(Business Plus, 2010).

22 **"permanently address the
structural issues presented"**:
"U.S. takes control of Fannie Mae
and Freddie Mac," by Edmund
L. Andrews, *New York Times,*
September 7, 2008. http://www.
nytimes.com/2008/09/07/busi-
ness/worldbusiness/07iht-trea-
sury.4.15955496.html

22 **"This is an opportunity to
get rid of institutions"**: "How Mr.
Volcker Would Fix It," by Gretchen
Morgenson, *New York Times,*
October 22, 2011.

http://www.nytimes.com/2011/
10/23/business/volckers-advice-
for-more-financial-reform.html

22 **"I believe that our housing
system should operate"**: "Remarks
by the President on Responsible
Homeownership," August 6, 2013.
https://www.whitehouse.gov/the-
press-office/2013/08/06/remarks-
president-responsible-homeown-
ership

22 **quite deliberately did not deal
with Fannie and Freddie:** "Why has
Congress left housing to Fannie Mae
and Freddie Mac?" by Neil Irwin,
Washington Post, March 5, 2013.
http://www.washingtonpost.com/
blogs/wonkblog/wp/2013/03/05/
why-has-congress-left-housing-
to-fannie-mae-and-freddie-mac/

22 **"The current state of the
GSEs can best be summed up"**: "A
Realistic Assessment of Housing
Finance Reform," by Laurie
Goodman, Urban Institute, August
18, 2004. http://www.urban.org/
sites/default/files/alfresco/publi-
cation-pdfs/413205-A-Realistic-
Assessment-of-Housing-Finance-
Reform.pdf

23 **some $5 trillion of securi-
ties outstanding:** "Fannie Mae and
Freddie Mac in Conservatorship,"
by Mark Jickling, Congressional
Research Service, September 15,
2008. http://fpc.state.gov/docu-
ments/organization/110097.pdf

23 **taking practically every penny of profit:** "Fannie Mae, Freddie Mac to send $6.8 bln to U.S. Treasury," by Lindsay Dunsmuir, *Reuters*, November 6, 2014. http://www.reuters.com/article/2014/11/06/usa-housing-idUSL1N-0SW0SS20141106

25 **"If you're not relevant, you're unprofitable":** "The Financial Crisis Inquiry Report," Financial Crisis Inquiry Commission, January 2011. http://www.gpo.gov/fdsys/pkg/GPO-FCIC/pdf/GPO-FCIC.pdf

27 **"opened the floodgates to the reckless private label":** Testimony of Joshua Rosner, U.S. House Financial Services Subcommittee on Capital Markets and Government Sponsored Enterprises, March 6, 2012. http://financialservices.house.gov/uploadedfiles/hhrg-113-ba16-wstate-jrosner-20130306.pdf

27 **a staggering 82 percent of sub-prime mortgages were refinanc-ings:** "Curbing Predatory Home Mortgage Lending: A Joint Report," Department of Treasury and Department of Housing and Urban Development, June 2000. http://archives.hud.gov/reports/treasrpt.pdf

28 **private-label issuance reached $1.15 trillion:** "The Financial Crisis Inquiry Report," Financial Crisis Inquiry Commission.

28 **a third of subprime mort-gages ... were used to buy homes:** "A House Is Not a Credit Card," by Bethany McLean, *New York Times*, November 13, 2014. http://www.nytimes.com/2014/11/14/opinion/a-house-is-not-a-credit-card.html

28 **homeowners cashed out approximately $966 billion:** "Housing Finance System: A Framework for Assessing Potential Changes," U.S. Government Accountability Office, October 7, 2014. http://gao.gov/products/GAO-15-131

29 **market share fell from 57 percent in 2003 to 42 percent in 2004:** "The Financial Crisis Inquiry Report," Financial Crisis Inquiry Commission.

29 **"customers who do not satisfy the stricter credit:** "Subprime Lending: Defining the Market and Its Customers," statement of the Coalition for Fair and Affordable Lending and New Century Financial Corporation, joint hearing of the Subcommittee on Housing and Community Opportunity and Subcommittee on Financial Institutions and Consumer Credit, March 30, 2004. http://financialservices.house.gov/media/pdf/033004st.pdf

30 **3.8 percent of subprime is-suance in 2001 ... 28.9 percent in 2005:** "The Effect of Large Investors on Asset Quality: Evidence from

154   Subprime Mortgage Securities,"
by Manuel Adelino, W. Scott
Frame, and Kristopher S. Gerardi,
April 2014. https://www.frbat-
lanta.org/research/publications/
wp/2014/14_04.aspx

31 "We face two stark choices":
"The Financial Crisis Inquiry
Report," Financial Crisis Inquiry
Commission.

**33 "Following the lead of Fed
chairman Alan Greenspan":** *The
Mortgage Wars: Inside Fannie Mae,
Big-Money Politics, and the Collapse
of the American Dream,* by Tim
Howard (McGraw-Hill, 2013).

34 "If you've got a bazooka": *On
the Brink: Inside the Race to Stop
the Collapse of the Global Financial
System,* by Henry Paulson.

**35 "Some of us who have helped
Fannie and Freddie":** Remarks by
Charles Schumer, the Brookings
Institution, December 19, 2007.
http://www.brookings.edu/~/me-
dia/events/2007/12/19-us-econo-
my/20071219_economy.pdf

**36 "The idea strikes me as
perverse":** "The Financial Crisis
Inquiry Report," Financial Crisis
Inquiry Commission.

**37 "Just maybe a bailout of Fannie
... would be a good thing":** "Is
Fannie Mae the Next Government
Bailout?" by Jonathan R. Laing,
Barron's, March 10, 2008.

http://online.barrons.com/articles/
SB120493962895621231

**37 "A government seizure is
inevitable":** "The Financial Crisis
Inquiry Report," Financial Crisis
Inquiry Commission.

**38 "Senior Bush administration
officials":** "U.S. Weighs Takeover of
Two Mortgage Giants," by Stephen
Labaton and Steven R. Weisman,
New York Times, July 11, 2008. http://
www.nytimes.com/2008/07/11/
business/11fannie.html

**39 "If the U.S. government al-
lows Fannie and Freddie to fail":**
"Freddie, Fannie Failure Could Be
World 'Catastrophe,' Yu Says," by
Kevin Hamlin, *Bloomberg,* August
22, 2008. http://www.bloomberg.
com/apps/news?pid=newsarchive&s
id=aslo2Eo1QVFI

**41 "prevent current shareholder
speculation":** Minutes to the
meeting of the Federal Accounting
Standards Advisory Board,
December 17, 2008. http://www.
fasab.gov/pdffiles/deco8mins.pdf

**42 "Treasury took advantage of
the 2008 financial":** "Treasury, the
Conservatorships and Mortgage
Reform," by Timothy Howard,
January 16, 2015. http://fanniemae-
shareholder.blogspot.com/2015/01/
treasury-conservatorships-and-
mortgage.html

42 **"They have to be used":**
"Fannie, Freddie to Buy $40 Billion a
Month of Troubled Assets," by Dawn
Kopecki, *Bloomberg*, October 11,
2008. http://www.bloomberg.com/
apps/news?sid=aDjJYMSphyMo&pi
d=newsarchive

43 **Foreign institutions ... owned
around $1 trillion:** "The Rescue of
Fannie Mae and Freddie Mac," by W.
Scott Frame, Andreas Fuster, Joseph
Tracy, and James Vickery, Federal
Reserve Bank of New York Staff
Reports, March 2015. http://www.
newyorkfed.org/research/staff_re-
ports/sr719.pdf

46 **"not deregulation, but dumb
regulation":** Jeb Hensarling's open-
ing statement at the Committee on
Financial Services hearing, January
27, 2015. http://financialservices.
house.gov/news/documentsingle.
aspx?DocumentID=398651

47 **31 million mortgages, or over
half:** *Hidden in Plain Sight: What
Really Caused the World's Worst
Financial Crisis and Why It Could
Happen Again*, by Peter Wallison
(Encounter Books, 2015).

49 **"I continue to think that
Peter overplays the mortgage is-
sue":** "An Examination of Attacks
Against the Financial Crisis Inquiry
Commission," Democratic Staff
Committee on Oversight and
Government Reform, July 13, 2011.

http://democrats.oversight.house.
gov/sites/democrats.oversight.
house.gov/files/documents/
FCIC%20Minority%20Report.pdf

49 **"I think wmt [William M.
Thomas] is going to push":** ibid.

51 **from 2005 to 2007, roughly
$2.9 trillion:** "Fannie, Freddie
and the Right Wing Myth of a
'Mortgage Meltdown,'" by David
Fiderer, February 7, 2015. http://
www.opednews.com/populum/
pagem.php?f=Fannie-Freddie-
and-the-Ri-by-David-Fiderer-
Freddie-Mac_Housing_Insolvency_
Meltdown-150207-203.html

54 **the FCIC archives at Stanford
University:** http://fcic.law.stanford.
edu/resource

54 **the best performers were
Fannie and Freddie:** Testimony
of Mark Zandi before the Senate
Banking Committee, September 12,
2013. https://www.economy.com/
getlocal?q=306BF929-5A1A-41FC-
9737-691E189D7D2F&app=eccafile

56 **wealthiest 40 percent of
borrowers:** "Changes in Buyer
Composition and the Expansion of
Credit During the Boom," by Manuel
Adelino, Antoinette Schoar, and
Felipe Severino, National Bureau
of Economic Research, January
2015. http://www.nber.org/papers/
w20848

156

58 **"What's good for American housing"**: "Fannie Mae's Last Stand," by Bethany McLean, *Vanity Fair*, February 2009. http://www.vanityfair.com/news/2009/02/fannie-and-freddie200902

59 **"attracts too little private capital"**: "Early Steps Down the Path of GSE Reform," by Jim Parrott, the Urban Institute, March 2015. http://www.urban.org/sites/default/files/alfresco/publication-pdfs/2000155-Early-Steps-Down-the-Path-of-GSE-Reform.pdf

60 **"scoring an executive post at Fannie Mae"**: "Nice work if you can get it: how Fannie Mae became Washington's biggest power player," by Michelle Cottle, *Washington Monthly*, June 1, 1998. http://www.thefreelibrary.com/Nice+work+if+you+can+get+it%3A+how+Fannie+Mae+became+Washington%27s...-a020789484

61 **"Fannie has this grandmotherly image"**: "Crony Capitalism: American Style," by Owen Ullmann, *The International Economy*, July/August 1999. http://www.international-economy.com/TIE_JA99_Ullmann.pdf

62 **Sarah Lehman Quinn's dissertation:** "Government Policy, Housing, and the Origins of Securitization, 1780–1968," by Sarah Lehman Quinn, 2010. https://escholarship.org/uc/item/7sq3f6xk

63 "Roosevelt Charges Federal Neglect of 'Little Fellow,'" *New York Times*† April 8, 1932. http://query.nytimes.com/gst/abstract.html?res=9907E3DC1431E633A2575BC0A9629C946394D6CF

65 **"extraordinarily difficult to try to compare"**: David Min's testimony at a hearing before the Committee on Financial Services, June 12, 2013. http://www.gpo.gov/fdsys/pkg/CHRG-113hhrg81763/html/CHRG-113hhrg81763.htm

71 **"one of the most powerful men in the United States"**: "The Big Chair; James Johnson, Head of Brookings, Fannie Mae and the Kennedy Center, Is in the Catbird Seat," by Lloyd Grove, Washington Post, March 27, 1998.

72 **"OFHEO was structurally weak and almost designed to fail"**: "The Financial Crisis Inquiry Report," Financial Crisis Inquiry Commission.

72 **"hobbled, muzzled, and underfed"**: "The Fall of Fannie Mae," by Bethany McLean, *Fortune,* January 24, 2005. http://archive.fortune.com/magazines/fortune/fortune_archive/2005/01/24/8234040/index.htm

82 **"extensive advertising has created"**: *Privatizing Fannie Mae, Freddie Mac and the Federal Home Loan Banks: Why and How*, by Peter J.

Wallison, Thomas H. Stanton, and
Bert Ely (AEI Press, 2004).

84 **"financing strategies fueled by
creativity"**: *All the Devils Are Here:
The Hidden History of the Financial
Crisis*, by Bethany McLean and Joe
Nocera (Portfolio, 2010).

85 **"He had a deep disdain"**:
On the Brink, by Henry Paulson,

86 **"to fend off possible future systemic difficulties"**:
Alan Greenspan's testimony
before the Committee on Banking,
Housing, and Urban Affairs,
February 24, 2004. http://www.
federalreserve.gov/boarddocs/
testimony/2004/20040224/

88 **"Frustrated by its inability
to win"**: "Regulators Hit Fannie,
Freddie With New Assault," by James
R. Hagerty and John D. McKinnon,
Wall Street Journal, April 28, 2004.
http://www.wsj.com/articles/
SB108310651573395309

89 **"These findings cannot be
explained"**: "Regulator Has No
Confidence in Fannie Leadership,"
by David S. Hilzenrath, *Washington
Post*, September 24, 2004. http://
www.washingtonpost.com/wp-dyn/
articles/A45910-2004Sep23.html

94 **"It was amazing how little
actual authority"**: *Stress Test:
Reflections on Financial Crises*, by
Timothy F. Geithner (Crown, 2014).

99 **"You have the power to help"**:   157
Letter from Timothy Geithner to Ed
DeMarco, July 31, 2012.
http://www.treasury.gov/connect/
blog/Pages/tfg-letter-demarco.aspx

99 "Is This Man Single-Handedly
Stifling the U.S. Housing Recovery?"
by Christopher Matthews, *Time*,
March 21, 2013. http://business.
time.com/2013/03/21/why-are-so-
many-lawmakers-and-ags-calling-
for-this-mans-job/

100 **"The magnitude of falsity,
conservatively measured, is enormous"**: "Judge's Ruling Against
2 Banks Finds Misconduct in '08
Crash," by Peter Eavis, *New York
Times*, May 11, 2015. http://www.
nytimes.com/2015/05/12/business/
dealbook/nomura-found-liable-in-
us-mortgage-suit-tied-to-finan-
cial-crisis.html

104 **"People who own Fannie and
Freddie debt"**: "Rep. Barney Frank
warns of Fannie, Freddie risks," by
Zachary A. Goldfarb, *Washington
Post*, March 6, 2010. http://www.
washingtonpost.com/wp-dyn/
content/article/2010/03/05/
AR2010030501764.html

106 **"This paper lays out
the Administration's plan"**:
"Reforming America's Housing
Finance Market: A Report to
Congress," Department of Treasury
and Department of Housing and
Urban Development, February 2011.

158   http://www.treasury.gov/initiatives/Documents/Reforming%20America%27s%20Housing%20Finance%20Market.pdf

111   **"will not be able to earn their way back":** Speech by Ed DeMarco, September 30, 2011. http://problembanklist.com/fhfa-head-says-fannie-mae-and-freddie-mac-cannot-be-fixed-0407/

112   *The Greatest Trade Ever: The Behind-the-Scenes Story of How John Paulson Defied Wall Street and Made Financial History,* by Gregory Zuckerman (Crown Business, 2009).

114   **"make clear the Administration's commitment":** "The Untouchable Profits of Fannie Mae and Freddie Mac," by Gretchen Morgenson, *New York Times,* February 15, 2014. http://www.nytimes.com/2014/02/16/business/the-untouchable-profits-of-fannie-mae-and-freddie-mac.html

118   **"Undoubtedly, rosy reporting":** "Revealing Fannie Mae's and Freddie Mac's Budget Costs: A Step Toward GSE Elimination," by Romina Boccia, The Heritage Foundation, March 16, 2014. http://www.heritage.org/research/reports/2014/03/revealing-fannie-maes-and-freddie-macs-budget-costs-a-step-toward-gse-elimination

124   **"the perpetual conservatorships":** "FHFA's Permanent Conservatorship Ignores the Law," by Michael H. Krimminger, *American Banker,* December 17, 2014. http://www.americanbanker.com/bankthink/fhfas-permanent-conservatorship-ignores-the-law-1071687-1.html

128   **"Investments in quality education":** "Michael Milken: How Housing Policy Hurts the Middle Class," by Michael Milken, *Wall Street Journal,* March 5, 2014. http://www.wsj.com/articles/SB10001424052702304610404579401613007521066

130   **"While housing usually leads the country out of recession":** "Obama to Outline Proposals to Bolster a Lagging Housing Sector," by Jonathan Weisman, *New York Times,* January 7, 2015. http://www.nytimes.com/2015/01/08/us/obama-to-outline-proposals-to-bolster-a-lagging-housing-sector.html

135   **"four core principles for what I believe reform should look like":** President Obama's remarks on homeownership, August 6, 2013. https://www.whitehouse.gov/the-press-office/2013/08/06/remarks-president-responsible-homeownership

141   **"The critical flaws in the legacy system":** Michael Stegman's remarks, March 5, 2015. http://www.treasury.gov/press-center/press-releases/Pages/jl9987.aspx

Columbia Global Reports is a publishing imprint from
Columbia University that commissions authors to
do original on-site reporting around the globe on a wide
range of issues. The resulting novella-length books
offer new ways to look at and understand the world that
can be read in a few hours. Most readers are curious
and busy. Our books are for them.

ALSO COMING IN FALL 2015
Little Rice: Smartphones, Xiaomi, and the Chinese Dream
Clay Shirky

The Cosmopolites: The Coming of the Global Citizen
Atossa Araxia Abrahamian

www.globalreports.columbia.edu

e **housing lobby likes to**
: "Life Without Fannie
ie," *Wall Street Journal*,
r 26, 2014. http://www.wsj.
cles/life-without-fannie-
die-1419635987

using for housing's sake":
etrou on Mortgages and
," by Karen Shaw Petrou,
Financial Analytics, June
2ohttp://www.fedfin.com/
og/β-karen-petrou-on-mort-
gages-d-medicare